CLOCK MAKING

FOR THE

WOODWORKER

BY WAYNE LOUIS KADAR

TAB BOOKS Inc.
BLUE RIDGE SUMMIT, PA. 17214

FIRST EDITION

FIRST PRINTING

Library of Congress Cataloging in Publication Data

Kadar, Wayne Louis.
Clock making for the woodworker.

Includes index.
1. Clock and watch making. 2. Woodwork. I. Title.
TS545.K33 1984   681.1'13   83-24125
ISBN 0-8306-0648-3
ISBN 0-8306-1648-9 (pbk.)

Contents

Acknowledgments

I N THIS LIFE THERE ARE FEW ACCOMPLISH-ments that are solely the work of one person. This book is no exception. There are many people who have been instrumental in this project, and they all should receive some recognition for their efforts.

First, I would like to thank my wife, Karen, and children who put up with the sleepless nights, mounds of scrap paper, and other major inconveniences while I wrote.

Klockit Company of Lake Geneva, Wisconsin, has graciously provided me with many of their movements, dials, and other clock hardware for photographic purposes. I am indebted to them for their assistance.

To name just a few more who were a help in the formation of this book are Paul Wojno for his design consultations and Ron Kramer for his woodworking abilities in assisting in construction. I would also like to thank the administration of Harbor Beach High School in conjunction with the use of school facilities.

The kind and understanding people of Oltz/ Hearsch Studio of Bad Axe, Michigan, need to receive credit for the miracles they performed on my black-and-white photographs.

I would also like to thank Lori Grezeszak for her many hours of editing, typing, proofreading, retyping, and patience. Without her help, this project would still be a few hundred pages of notebook paper in the blue, three-ring binder marked "The Book."

Introduction

CRAFTSMEN INVOLVED WITH CLOCK CONSTRUC-tion do not have the luxury of a large amount of printed plans from which to build. There are a few companies who sell clock plans, but the purchase price of the plans often exceeds the price of the wood necessary to build the finished product. This book presents to the craftsman a variety of clock styles (modern traditional, replica, wall, desk, and mantel) at a fraction of the price of individual plans.

The clocks described in this book have been designed with the ease of construction as the main consideration. Most of the time-consuming jointery historically used in clock cabinet construction has been substituted with simple butt joints reinforced with corner blocks. This is possible, in part, because of the improvements made in wood adhesives. The construction has been simplified in this manner to place the art of clock building within reach of the craftsman who does not have the experience or access to woodworking machines necessary for fine joinery. The craftsman who does have access to the woodworking machines and

knowledge of joinery, has the option of adapting the plans to incorporate such woodworking techniques as might be desired.

In this book, the clocks have been categorized into four groups. First are the kitchen clocks specifically designed to fit into the decorating scheme of the food preparation area. Next are mantel and desk clocks. This chapter contains clocks that are traditionally found on the fireplace mantel or small clocks that will grace the desk of the business person or student.

Because most clocks can be found hanging on a wall, the majority of the clocks in this book fall into the chapter on wall clocks. Clocks were traditionally hung on a wall to allow room for weight shells to drop and pendulums to swing. Today they remain mounted on the wall for convenience.

The fourth group of clocks has been designed around the battery clock movement. The development of the battery-operated movement has opened an imaginative door for clock designers. Clocks no longer need to be wound, weight shells do not have to be reset, nor does the clock need to be tethered to an outlet by an unsightly electrical cord. The battery movement provides a reliable clock movement that can produce easily made clocks with an individualized distinctive appearance. All that is required is to drill a hole through the clock face, insert a battery movement, and insert some type of hour markers. The twenty-one clocks in the chapter are just the tip of the iceberg. The design possibilities are endless. Let your imagination guide you into the world of quick, but impressive clocks.

The accessibility to clock movements has been another stumbling block for the craftsman. A large selection of movements simply just were not available. The marketing of clock movements to the home craftsman is a recent development that has grown to include many fine mail-order companies. A list of many of these companies can be found in the Suppliers section. These mail-order companies sell a wide range of supplies needed by the craftsman. There are many types of movements (weight or spring driven, electric, and battery), dials, bezels, hands, and hardware.

Clock construction has long been reserved for the commercial manufacturers of clock cabinets. The art was a mystery to the average home craftsman. This book, and the mail-order, clock-supply companies, prove to the woodworking public that they too can create beautiful clocks that can be displayed with pride and passed down from generation to generation with honor.

Chapter 1

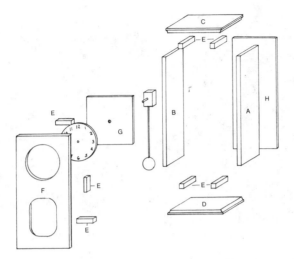

Clock-Construction Tools

THIS CHAPTER DESCRIBES SOME TOOLS THAT CAN be used by the craftsman when building the clocks in this book. The description of each concentrates on the safe use of the tool and how its use applies to clock construction. The information is brief. If more information is required, there are many fine books available that deal exclusively with the topic of tools and their use.

The tools have been grouped into categories as to the function they perform. The categories are then listed in the approximate order in which they might be used in clock construction. It must be remembered that the order of the list is only a guide, not the gospel.

SAFETY

Any tool used in clock construction, be it hand or power operated, has the potential to harm its operator or those nearby. With this in mind, the craftsman must approach each tool with an eye toward safety. Remember that wood is much harder than skin. A tool designed to cut, shave, or shape wood will most definitely have no trouble causing injury.

Another characteristic of wood that requires special safety attention is that when cut, splinters have a tendency to fly away from the surface. The operator should always wear eye protection while working.

MEASURING TOOLS

There are few tools more necessary in the wood-working shop than those used for measuring. The selection of measuring instruments available at a hardware store can be overwhelming. When selecting a measuring tool, look for one that is accurate, easy to read, and is of a high enough quality to endure much use.

Some of the types available are the tape measure, the bench rule, and the zigzag rule. The tape measure is a flexible thin blade that rolls up into its own case. It can be purchased in several lengths from 4 feet to 80 or 100 feet. No shop should be without one of these tapes (Fig. 1-1).

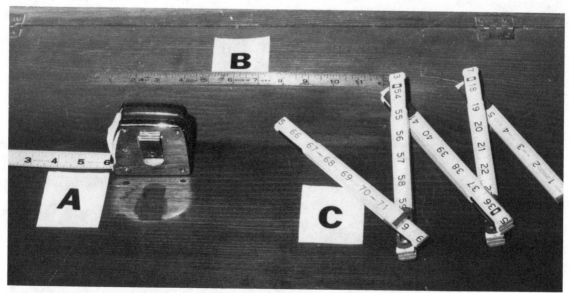

Fig. 1-1. The three types of measuring instruments commonly found in a woodshop: (A) tape measure, (B) steel or bench rule, (C) zigzag rule.

Fig. 1-2. Handsaws used in the shop are of three basic types: (A) rip saw, (B) coping saw, (C) crosscut saw.

The bench rule is made of steel. It has the inch markings permanently engraved in it. These are very accurate and handy to have in the shop. They are available in 1-, 2-, or 3-foot lengths.

The zig-zag rule was used extensively in the past, but is being replaced by the tape measure.

SAWS

Saws should be divided into three subcategories. These are handsaws, portable power saws, and stationary power saws. A handsaw operates by the blade being pushed across the board. The most common types of handsaws are the crosscut and ripsaws. The crosscut is used, as the name indicates, to cut across the grain of the wood. When cutting in the same direction which the grain runs, a ripsaw should be used (Fig. 1-2).

The crosscut saw and the ripsaw can only make straight cuts. In order to cut curves in wood, a coping saw should be used. The coping saw has a U-shaped frame and a thin, replaceable blade that allows it to cut irregular shapes.

Over the years, portable power saws have been developed that operate in the same manner as their hand-operated counterparts. The portable electric circular saw is used to cut wood with and against the grain—the same as the handsaws—but much faster (Fig. 1-3).

Where the coping saw is the handsaw for cutting curves, the scroll saw is its portable power brother. The scroll saw (jigsaw) has a small blade that functions in an up-and-down cutting operation.

The next subcategory of saws is the stationary power machines. The machines differ from the

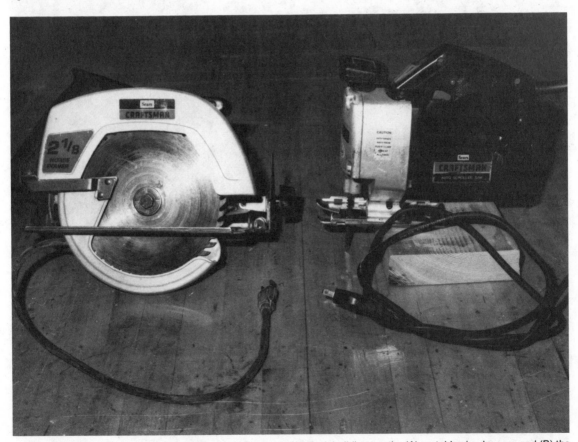

Fig. 1-3. Two portable power saws that help the craftsman in his clock building are the (A) portable circular saw, and (B) the saber or jigsaw.

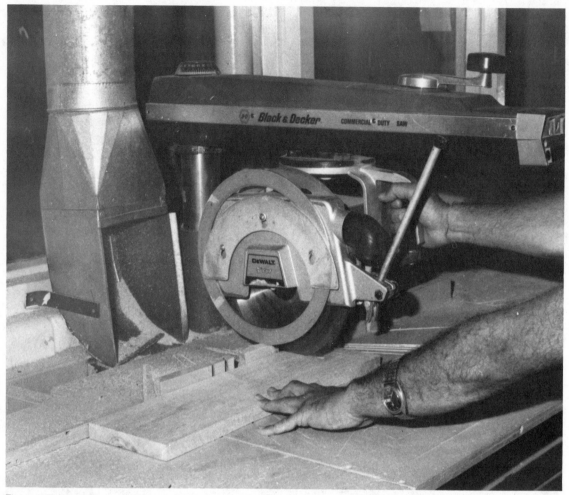

Fig. 1-4. The radial-arm saw is a stationary saw that can be used for most sawing operations.

other types of saws in that the hand and portable saws were taken to the wood. Here the wood is taken to the saw. The machines are capable of much more accurate work than is possible with the other saws.

The radial-arm saw, or cutoff saw, has been designed to function primarily in a crosscutting capacity. Because crosscutting is not the only operation necessary in most wood projects, the saw is also capable of ripping, cutting miters and compound miters, rabbeting, and dadoing—to name the most common (Fig. 1-4).

The primary function of the table saw is for cutting in the same direction as the grain (Fig. 1-5).

Nevertheless, this saw can also be used to perform the same functions listed for the radial-arm saw.

The jigsaw has been designed to cut curves in wood (Fig. 1-6). It uses a blade similar to that of the coping saw. It functions in the same manner except that with the jigsaw the wood is pressed against the blade, and in the hand operation the coping saw is pressed against the wood.

SHAPING TOOLS

A rasp is an extremely course file that is used to remove large amounts of material quickly. The rasp is strictly a shaping tool; it is not a smoothing tool. It leaves a rough surface (Fig. 1-7).

Once the initial shaping has been done with a rasp, the rough surface must be worked with a series of wood files. The coarse files are used first, working toward a finer file to smoothly produce the desired shape.

DRILLING TOOLS

Clock construction requires the drilling of at least one hole in almost any clock that is built (the hole which the movement hand-shaft fits through). The hole can be drilled by either hand or power drills.

The brace and bit, although no longer found in production use, is still quite a handy tool when used on softer woods. The drill bits used with a brace are required to have an enlarged square shank. These bits cannot be used in any other type of drill (Fig. 1-8).

The hand drill is a helpful tool for drilling holes in wood. Any bit except the brace bit can be used,

providing it fits into the chuck.

If there are many holes to be drilled, the two previously mentioned methods will become quite tiring and time consuming. An electric drill can make the job much easier. The portable electric drill can be purchased at any hardware, discount, or department store that sells tools. The prices range from under $20 to in the hundreds of dollars. The more expensive ones are usually heavy-duty models used by professional woodworkers. The size of portable electric drills is determined by the largest size drill bit that will fit into the chuck. Common sizes are ¼ inch, ⅜ inch, and ½ inch.

ADHESIVES

While working with wood in the field of clock construction, it is often necessary to glue two or more boards together. There are many types of glue available that are capable of performing this func-

Fig. 1-5. The table saw is one of the most useful of all stationary saws. Although it is expensive initially, it is necessary for the craftsman who intends to produce clocks in large numbers for resale.

Fig. 1-6. The jigsaw is another stationary saw that is very useful in the shop. Its thin blade allows it to cut curves in wood, much the same as the coping saw does.

tion. Regardless of the type of glue selected, it is important that the directions be read and followed.

There are four main types of glue that will prove to be satisfactory for clock construction. The first is polyvinyl acetate glue, sometimes called white glue. This is the most common type of glue used in woodworking. It is available under many brand names at most stores. Although it is white in color, it sets quickly under clamp pressure to a transparent finish. The glue should only be used for interior uses because it does not have resistance to water.

Aliphatic resin glue, often called yellow glue, is currently becoming quite a popular glue with woodworkers. Its major attributes are that it is stronger and sets faster than its white glue counterpart. The yellow glue is also available at many retail

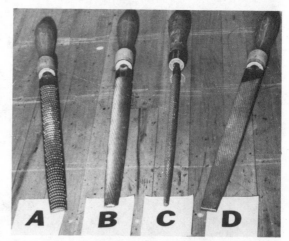

Fig. 1-7. The rasp (A) and files are examples of those available for the craftsman's use: (B) a half-round file, (C) a rattail or round file, and (D) a flat file.

6

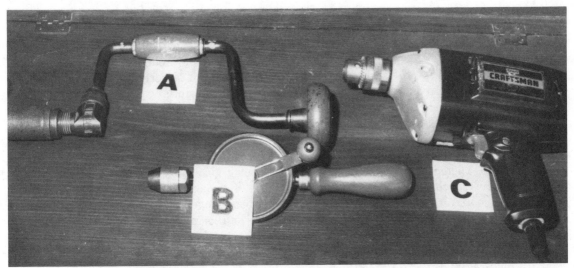

Fig. 1-8. Three examples of tools used for drilling holes in wood are a brace (A), a hand drill (B), and an electric drill (C).

outlets under many brand names. Their names will usually refer to the fact that they are especially designed for use in woodworking.

The first two types of glue are not waterproof.

Moisture will slowly deteriorate the glue. If the glue is to be used on a project that will be used on the exterior, a resorcinol resin glue is recommended. This glue is usually available in two parts.

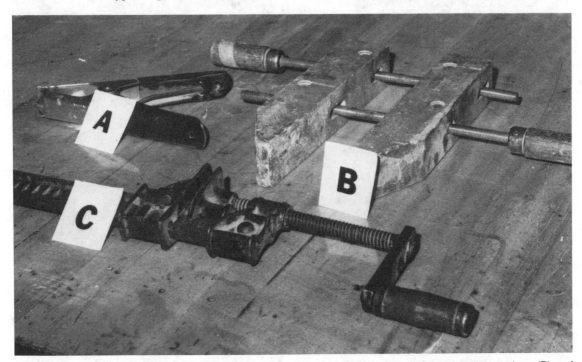

Fig. 1-9. Three commercially produced clamps used in woodworking are the spring clamp (A), the hand-screw clamp (B), and the bar clamp (C).

One part is a fine powder that is mixed with the other part, a liquid. The glue is not fast-setting, but it is waterproof enough to be used in wooden boat construction.

Unlike the adhesives previously discussed, contact cement does not require the use of clamps while the glue sets. The glue is applied to both surfaces. After the cement has dried, the two parts are placed in contact with each other. As the two coated surfaces touch, they instantly become bonded together. There is no room for error when you are using contact cement.

There are more varieties of glue than the four previously mentioned, but these are the most popular and tend to do the best job. White and yellow glues are the two recommended for use in clock construction because they have all of the characteristics that are required for clock cabinets. They are not waterproof, but then most wood clock cabinets are not subjected to large or consistent amounts of moisture.

CLAMPS

Clamps can be referred to as any tool that applies pressure to two or more pieces of wood while they are being glued together. A clamp can take the shape of a complicated bar clamp used for gluing wide panels together or as simple as a weight that is placed on a board to hold it in place. Examples of the latter can be gallon cans of paint or cement blocks.

Fig. 1-10. Abrasive paper is available in varying grades of coarseness. The more coarse the paper, the faster the wood is cut. Finer paper is used to smooth the wood surface.

Most woodworkers will have at their access either spring, hand-screw, or bar clamps (Fig. 1-9). The spring clamp is the most handy of the three. It is used to clamp wood together (although they do not apply very much pressure). The hand-screw clamp is most commonly used in woodshops to apply pressure to glued surfaces. The hand-screw clamp is very good, but it does have its limitations. The two parallel jaws of the clamp will only open so far. When this is a problem, the bar clamp is the tool to use. The bar clamp is available in sizes ranging from 24 inches long to 48 inches and longer. This type clamp is adjustable from a few inches to several feet; this makes it quite useful in the home shop.

A method for applying pressure to two or more glued boards is necessary in the construction of clock cabinets. This method can take the shape of any of those mentioned above. What is important is that an even pressure be applied to the glued surfaces for a duration long enough to promote good setting of the glue.

ABRASIVES

Abrasives are commonly known as sandpaper. The use of sandpaper in sanding a wood project is often looked upon as a necessary evil. It is a job that needs to be done to produce a smooth defect-free surface. Yet this is a job that is time consuming and tedious.

Sandpaper is available in many grades ranging from coarse to very fine. There has been a numerical system developed by the industry that applies a large number to fine papers and progressively lowering numbers as the grades become more coarse. An 80-grit paper is considered a coarse paper and it cuts wood faster than a finer abrasive paper. When wood has been ridded of major defects with the 80-grit paper, a 120 or 150 grit, a medium grade, should be used. A fine paper is used next to smooth the wood surface. The fine paper will have a grit number of 220 to 320 (Fig. 1-10).

Tools have been developed out of necessity and improved and perfected over the years. The craftsman no longer needs to make all cuts and joints with hand tools. He has at his access many accurate power tools that reduce the amount of time necessary to complete the operation.

The tools that have been described in this chapter are part of the craftsman heritage. Learn to use your tools, care for them, and respect them. They can be old friends or deadly enemies.

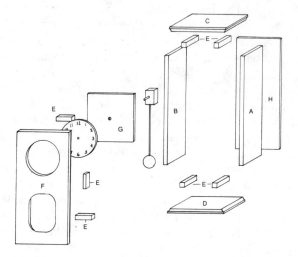

Chapter 2

Clock Movements

T HE BEAUTIFUL CLOCK CABINET—WITH ITS graceful flowing lines, a handsome dial, and ornate hands—is nothing without the clock movement. The movement is the veritable heart of the clock. This chapter answers many questions that will crop up while you are building clocks.

WEIGHT-DRIVEN MOVEMENT

The source of power for the first clocks was gravity pulling on weight shells (Fig. 2-1). The weights, usually two rocks, were suspended on ropes that were wound around an axle within the clock. The axle turned—setting into motion a series of gears—causing the single time-indicating hand to revolve. The biggest drawback of this clock was its lack of accuracy. Considering that these first mechanical clocks were developed using the technology available almost 400 years ago, it was quite a mechanical accomplishment.

The weight shells hanging from the movement does limit its use in some styles of clocks. The clock cabinet must allow enough space beneath the

movement for the dropping action of the weight shells (Fig. 2-2). Another factor to consider when selecting this movement is that every few days the weights must be reset or the clock will stop. If the design of your clock calls for a pendulum and you prefer the appearance of hanging weight shells, this will be your best choice of movement. If a battery movement is to be used, dummy weight shells can be hung from the cabinet to provide the illusion of a weight-driven movement.

SPRING-DRIVEN MOVEMENT

Early clocks were heavy and bulky and that made moving them virtually impossible. To allow the clock some degree of mobility, a portable method of propulsion was needed. In the fifteenth century the spring-driven movement was developed (Fig. 2-3). This type of movement no longer required a dropping weight to propel it. Instead it was powered by a coiled spring that could release its wound-up energy at a controlled slow pace (although the spring required rewinding at intervals). The clocks

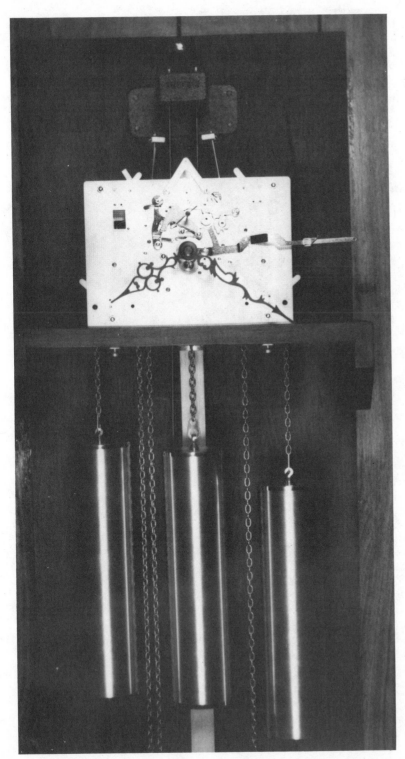

Fig. 2-1. An example of a weight-driven clock movement (courtesy of Klockit).

Fig. 2-2. Clock cabinet size required to house a weight-driven movement (courtesy of Klockit).

Fig. 2-3. A spring-driven movement showing a windup key and chime rods (courtesy of Klockit).

made in this manner were much smaller. For the first time, mechanical clocks became portable. The problem with early spring-driven movements was their accuracy. They were not even as accurate as the weight-driven movements of the day, but they did permit a certain amount of portability.

The major breakthrough that increased the accuracy of the spring-driven and weight-driven movements was the development of the pendulum escapement. The Italian scientist Galileo determined that a swinging object will swing the same distance from center to the right as it swings from the center to the left. He also realized that the length of the pendulum determined the distance the bottom of the pendulum would travel. In his later years, Galileo designed a clock escapement that used the pendulum principle to regulate time, but he never built a working model.

The Dutch astronomer Christian Huygens was the first to build a clock using a pendulum escapement. This greatly improved the accuracy of the time-keeping instruments. By the middle of the seventeenth century, pendulum clocks had achieved a reputation of being accurate to within seconds a day. Even clocks built earlier were being retrofitted with a pendulum.

The spring-driven movements produced today are expectantly much better than their predecessors. An improved, efficient method of escapement

Fig. 2-5. A battery movement used in many commercially produced and home-produced clocks.

is used, and modern metallurgy has given us springs that eliminate the possibility of overwinding (the cause of many damaged early spring clock movements).

Spring-driven movements are fine for smaller wall clocks, and especially mantel and table clocks. A key is used to wind up the spring that operates the clock. On clocks that have a chiming mechanism, there is usually a separate spring that runs it.

ALTERNATING ELECTRICAL-CURRENT MOVEMENT

Alternating current (ac) is the type of electricity brought into the house and used with wall outlets. Shortly after the use of electricity became wide spread, electric clocks came into existence (Fig. 2-4). The clock was readily accepted by the masses because of the lack of maintenance it required. There was no longer a need to regularly reset weights or remember to wind up the spring. This type of clock was not as versatile as other clocks because it is shackled to an electrical outlet. To work, it will always need to be near a source of

Fig. 2-4. An electric clock movement minus the clock cabinet.

electricity and must be connected by a cord.

Despite this inconvenience, the movement is one of the most widely used and accurate of all clock movements. Just about every house in this country has at least one electric alarm clock. Barring any blackouts, this type of clock movement will accurately serve its owners for many years without maintenance.

BATTERY-DRIVEN MOVEMENT

As people became more style-conscious about the decor of their home, they did not appreciate having the electrical power cord hanging from their clocks. This problem could be solved by installing an electrical outlet behind the clock. This is done most easily during new construction or when major remodeling is being done. For the most part, however, the expense involved was prohibitive.

The logical answer to this problem was a battery-operated movement (Fig. 2-5). This is a clock movement that operates on stored electrical energy in a battery. The battery movement has all of the advantages of the ac electric clock mechanism and many of its own. Power outages will not affect it, and there is no unsightly power cord to hinder its appearance. These movements can supply the time accurate to within a few seconds a year. The battery will only have to be changed about once a year.

The role of the battery movement has enlarged from its beginning to the present. The early movements were simple, inaccurate mechanical devices. Today this inexpensive style of movement has advanced to remarkable heights. There are battery-powered quartz movements, pendulum movements of all lengths, electronic chiming movements, chime rod, and hammer movements—just to name some of this movement's advantages (Fig. 2-6).

There are many factors that should be considered when selecting a movement for your clocks. If you have not already made your decision based solely on personal preference, the following information details several factors that should be taken into consideration when making this decision.

How Much Money Do You Want to Spend?

Because the weight- and spring-driven movements

Fig. 2-6. A battery-powered chiming movement (courtesy of Klockit).

tend to be expensive, this is probably a very important consideration. These movements require more gears and more expensive materials.

The battery-operated movements of the day are available in a wide price range (depending on the features they have). There are less expensive models that can be purchased for a small amount of money, while the more accurate quartz movements are accordingly more expensive. Perhaps you want the look of a weight-driven unit at the price of a battery movement. This is no problem because weight shells can be hung from the battery movement case. These shells will not be functional, but they give the appearance of being so (Fig. 2-7).

Does the Clock Need a Pendulum?

The pendulum was once a functional part of the timepiece. In several of the movements available today, it is still vital to the keeping of time. Most modern spring-driven and weight-driven movements rely on the pendulum as an escapement, (although there are several that do not). There are

Fig. 2-7. A clock movement shown with nonfunctional weight shells.

also battery movements that combine the advantages of a battery power source and the appearance of a pendulum (Fig. 2-8).

Is Extreme Accuracy Necessary?

The weight-driven and wind-up movements available these days are by far more accurate than those used by earlier craftsmen. These clock mechanisms allow for a certain amount of adjustments, but it can be a tedious job to achieve a high degree of accuracy. Nevertheless by following the manufacturer's instructions and keeping your patience, you can obtain an accurate timepiece.

A recent development now available is the quartz-crystal battery movement. This type of movement has been developed using some of the technological advances found in the wristwatch industry. The quartz oscillates at an even measure of time, breaking up a second into many smaller units, allowing a high degree of accuracy. The quartz movement is expensive, but it is very accurate and dependable.

Should the Clock Chime?

A clock that chimes is an option available on clocks powered by any of the three sources. The weight-driven and wind-up movements come in two main chimes: Winchester and gong strike.

The Winchester is probably the most familiar of all chimes. It sounds a fourth of its total chime at the quarter hour, half at the half hour, three quarters at quarter to the hour, and the full Winchester chime of the hour-along with counting out the hour (Fig. 2-9).

The gong strike sounds once on the half hour and counts out the hour on the hour.

Fig. 2-8. A battery-operated movement.

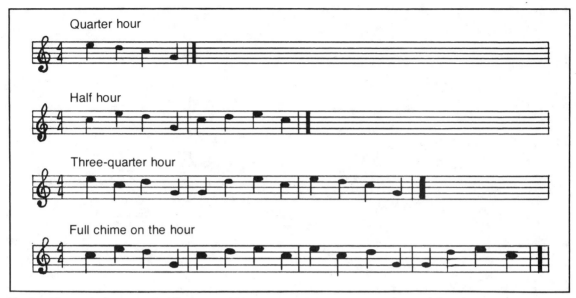

Fig. 2-9. The musical score to the Winchester chime.

The battery movement that chimes is a relatively new development and is available from most distributors. Battery chimes are offered in both the hammer and chime rod, and also the electronic chime.

The quality of the sound of the chimes is determined by the type of chime used. Many large grandfather clock type of movements use tuned chime tubes. These make a beautiful mellow tone, but they are rather expensive. Another type of chime is the chime rod (Fig. 2-10). These also can produce beautiful sounds; it depends on the material used in the rods. Always attempt to hear the chimes before purchasing the movement; of course when you order by mail this cannot be done.

A feature that is sometimes available with battery, weight-driven, and wind-up movements is a switch to turn off the chimes. This can be very important to those people who are light sleepers and do not appreciate being awakened every half hour. The craftsman building for resale should be sure to point out this feature to prospective customers; it could clinch the sale.

What about Movement Size?

An important consideration to study while selecting the correct movement is the size of the movement. When the size is neglected it results in a disaster. When selecting the movement, regardless of its motivating force, analyze the dimensions in the clock suppliers catalog (see clock material suppliers chapter) to ensure the movement will fit into

Fig. 2-10. A windup movement showing the chime rods.

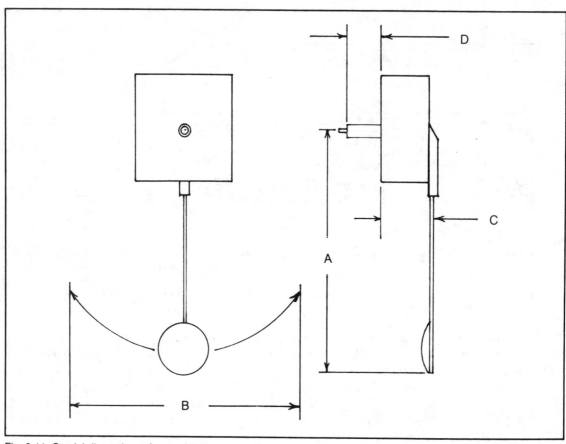

Fig. 2-11. Crucial dimensions of a pendulum movement.

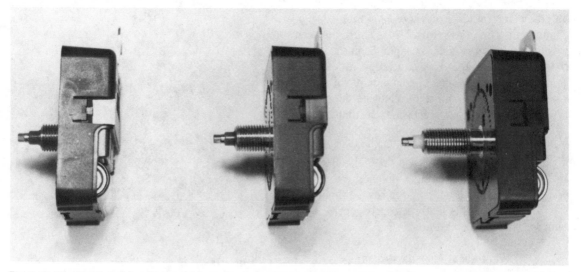

Fig. 2-12. The hand-shaft lengths available on clock movements (courtesy of Klockit).

the clock case. In many of the clock plans in this book, the size of the clock movement cavity or cabinet can be enlarged to some extent to house slightly larger movements.

Movements with pendulums pose special problems for fitting a movement with the cabinet. There are four crucial measurements that must be considered (Fig. 2-11). One is the pendulum length (A of Fig. 2-11). This length is measured from the center of the hand-shaft to the bottom of the pendulum bob. The pendulum swing is the maximum distance the pendulum travels from side to side (B of Fig. 2-11). The clock cabinet interior size must

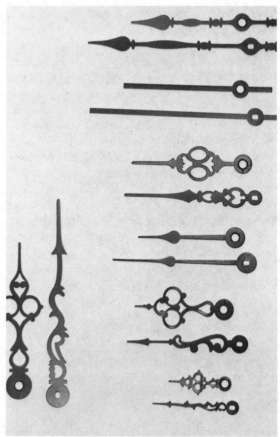

Fig. 2-14. Examples of common hands available from most clock wholesalers.

have a width larger than this size so that it will not interfere with the pendulum movement. Another crucial dimension is the distance from the clock movement front to the pendulum shaft (C of Fig. 2-11). This usually does not create a problem, but it might come into play when designing clocks.

The final crucial dimension is the hand-shaft length (D of Fig. 2-11). This is not only important on pendulum clocks, but on all clock movements. Figure 2-12 shows three of the most common hand-shaft lengths. Movement A is for dials up to ¼ of an inch thick, B for ⅜-inch thick dials, and C for dials up to ¾ of an inch thick.

THE HANDS

Modern clocks would be worthless if they did not

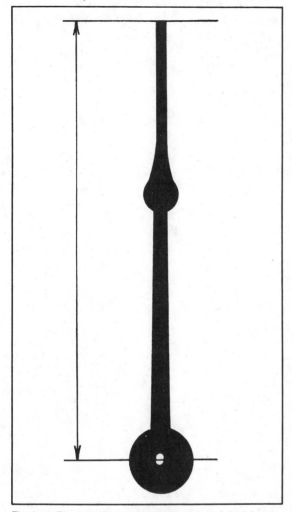

Fig. 2-13. The manufacturer's measurement of clock hands.

have hands (excluding the digital models). Most clock suppliers give a free pair of hands with the sale of each movement. The free hands, however, might not be the style that fits your clock cabinet. Heavy, black hands that look like a reproduction from a clock built in the 1700s would not look right on a modernistic wall clock. If you want hands other than those supplied with the movement, most suppliers will allow you to make a substitution at little or no cost. Hands generally can be purchased in either black or brass finishes. If another color is preferred, a can of spray paint can be used.

Because hands come in several lengths, make sure you order the proper size for your dial. If you order the movement, dial, and hands from the same supplier—and tell them they will be used to-gether—the supplier will make certain that they are all compatible. Clock hands are measured from the center of the hand-shaft mounting hole to the tip of the minute hand (Fig. 2-13).

If the hands are ordered separately and the correct size is unknown, the following is a rule-of-thumb that you can follow. The minute hand should be slightly longer than the distance from the center of the dial to the center of the hour markers. The hour hand should be noticeably shorter than the minute hand, but should not extend past the hour markers. Most hands are designed so that a small amount can be cut off if they are too long.

Most suppliers offer a wide variety of styles and sizes of hands. Shown in Fig. 2-14 are examples of some hands that are available.

Chapter 3

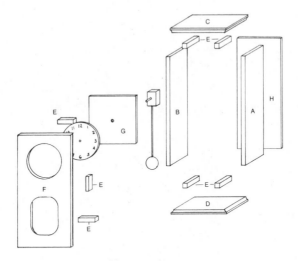

The Dial or Clock Face

ONCE THE SELECTION OF MOVEMENT AND hands has been made, the next point to consider is what type of dial or face you will want to use for the clock. Because the face is the focal point of any clock, it is important that care be taken when you decide what materials to use. There are many materials and styles at your disposal.

COMMERCIALLY PRODUCED DIALS

The easiest and the most expensive dials are those that can be purchased through the mail-order companies that specialize in clocks and clock supplies. These dials are beautifully produced from materials such as brass, porcelain, aluminum, or paper. The major disadvantage of using commercially produced dials is the cost. Etched, ornate clock faces such as those commonly found on large grandfather clocks can cost upwards to $50. Dials printed on paper can be purchased for less than a few dollars. There are also many companies that offer an extensive selection of medium-priced dials (Fig. 3-1).

Many of the companies that sell clock supplies list the sizes of their dials or hour markers in both metric and Arabic dimensions. Unfortunately, there are a few of the suppliers that only provide the size in metrics. Unless you are familiar with metrics, this could pose a problem when selecting a dial to fit a clock cabinet. For the convenience of the craftsman, Fig. 3-2 is a conversion chart. The figures in the chart are the sizes for the most common dials.

The craftsman building for resale might find it advantageous to use commercially produced dials. Even though it will cost more it will save time. These dials also help to give a homemade clock a professional look.

DIAL AND BEZEL

There is a commercially produced dial that is available through clock suppliers that has a dial and glass bezel. The dial will be a paper or metal dial with printed or painted hour ring and markers and a convex glass that covers the dial (Fig. 3-3). There

Fig. 3-1. A variety of commercially produced dials (courtesy of Klockit).

is also a metal or plastic trim band around the glass. The bezel is generally hinged so that it can be lifted to set the time or to wind the movement. The dial and bezel is desirable on various clocks (including some mantel and wall clocks). The marine chronometer and Brookfield clocks would look best with this type of dial and bezel setup (Fig. 3-4).

Some clocks require a dial that is purchased commercially simply because it would not look right any other way. One example is the Connecticut shelf clock (Fig. 3-5). On the other hand, there are clocks that would not look good with a beautifully produced dial.

HOUR MARKERS

If you do not want to use the commercially produced dials, what is the alternative? There are many other methods that can be employed to mark the hours on the clock face. The clock supply companies offer many types of numbers, dots, and dashes to mark

Conversion Chart	
3¼″ = 81 MM	8¼″ = 208 MM
4″ = 100 MM	9″ = 227 MM
4¼″ = 107 MM	9½″ = 240 MM
5″ = 125 MM	9⅝″ = 243 MM
5¼″ = 132 MM	9⅞″ = 250 MM
5½″ = 139 MM	10″ = 253 MM
5¾″ = 145 MM	10¼″ = 260 MM
5⅞″ = 148 MM	10¾″ = 271 MM
6″ = 153 MM	11″ = 278 MM
6⅛″ = 154 MM	11¼″ = 284 MM
6¼″ = 157 MM	11½″ = 291 MM
6½″ = 164 MM	11¾″ = 297 MM
6⅝″ = 167 MM	12″ = 304 MM
6¾″ = 170 MM	12¼″ = 310 MM
6⅞″ = 174 MM	12⅝″ = 319 MM
7″ = 177 MM	12⅞″ = 326 MM
7½″ = 189 MM	13″ = 330 MM
7¾″ = 196 MM	13¼″ = 336 MM
7⅞″ = 200 MM	13½″ = 342 MM
8″ = 202 MM	13¾″ = 349 MM

Fig. 3-2. A metric-to-standard conversion chart.

Fig. 3-3. A glass bezel and dial (courtesy of Klockit).

the hours. These are usually molded of high-quality plastic and come in either all black, or gold with a black background (Fig. 3-6). Some suppliers also offer markers made of polished brass in the shape of Roman numerals, Arabic numbers, dots, dashes, and even in the signs of the zodiac (Fig. 3-7).

Most of these items are equipped with some method to apply the marker to the clock face. They might have a thumbtack type point to be pushed into the wood, while others are preglued to stick to the surface. If they have none of these, the markers can be applied to the wood—after the finish has been applied—by using a quality glue. The best glue to use is one that dries clear in case it squeezes out from under the markers. If you are using plastic markers, a recommended glue to use is the type used on plastic models. To apply the brass markers, it is best to use one of the two-part epoxy glues on the market. This type of glue will adhere almost any

Fig. 3-4. A marine chronometer and traditional mantel clock with a dial and bezel setup (courtesy of Klockit).

Fig. 3-5. The Connecticut shelf clock with a commercially produced dial (dial courtesy of Klockit).

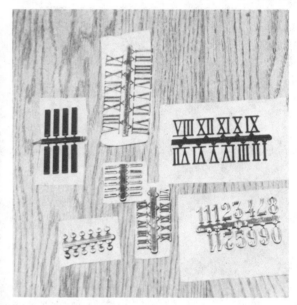

Fig. 3-6. Examples of plastic hour markers available through clock mail-order houses (courtesy of Klockit).

material to another.

There are many ways to mark the hours on a clock other than buying commercially produced materials. Depending on the type of clock and the decor of the room in which it is to be placed, many items found around the house or shop can be used as markers.

Nails can be used easily for hour markers. They do not require messy glue to hold them. There is a style of nail that will blend with almost any decor. Finish or casing nails of any size can be used for the hour markers. An interesting effect can be produced by pounding in two nails at the 12, 3, 6, and 9 hour positions and one nail at the remaining hour marks (Fig. 3-8).

To give the clock an early American appearance, cut nails can be used. Cut nails are the type used to nail wood to concrete; they have a thick,

rectangular head. Another nail that creates an interesting effect is the horseshoe nail. This adds a rugged, rustic appearance. Horseshoe nails can still be purchased through some mail-order catalogs.

Fig. 3-7. Solid brass hour markers (courtesy of Klockit).

Fig. 3-8. A clock face using finish nails as hour markers.

There are many types of ornamental nails available at your local hardware store (Fig. 3-9).

Carpet stores have nails that are used to hold down the metal threshold plates that separate a carpeted room from one that is not. The nails come in chrome, brass, and copper colors. A mixture of colors, or just one of them, can be used to create an unusual clock face. Plumbers often use copper nails to hold pipe supports to stud walls. These nails are a bright copper color and might be the type of hour marker you need to match your decor.

Hardware stores or upholstery shops have ornamental thumbtacks or upholstery tacks that are used to attach the fabric to the wood frame of the furniture. There are many styles available, some round, square, flat, oval, smooth, or with a brushed finish. One of these styles is sure to make hour markers that will complement the face of your clock.

There are, of course, many objects that can be used to mark the hours of a clock (anything from sea shells to simply drilling holes at each point—larger holes at the 12, 3, 6, 9, and smaller ones at the others). See Fig. 3-10. Always be on the lookout for materials that can be used in your clock-making endeavors. How about bottle caps from 12 different kinds of beer or pop? This could be the makings of a great clock for the recreation room.

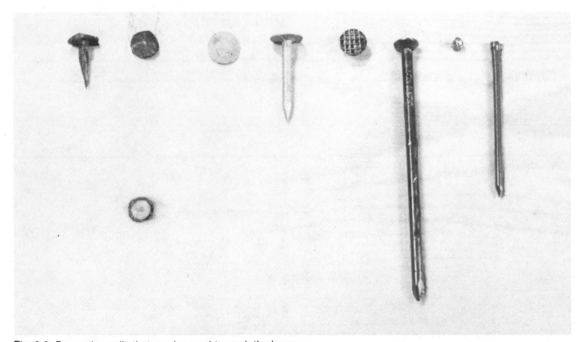

Fig. 3-9. Decorative nails that can be used to mark the hours.

Fig. 3-10. Marking the hours by drilling a hole in the clock face.

LOCATING HOUR POSITIONS

Until the advent of the digital clock, the face of the clock has remained relatively unchanged. There have been some improvements and modifications, but for the most part the clock face is the same as it has been for centuries. We are all familiar with the conventional clock face with the 12 on top, 3 at the right, 6 below, and 9 at the left of center. But setting up this face on a piece of wood is not one of the easiest jobs—unless you know how.

The simplest method to lay out the hour marks is by using a protractor. A protractor is a thin plastic or metal half-moon shaped tool that is used to measure angles (Fig. 3-11). One can be purchased for a moderate price at any store that sells school supplies.

To use a protractor, it is important that the center hole—the hole where the hand shaft of the movement comes through the face—is located first. This point is where you will set the middle point of the protractor.

With a protractor set in this position, draw a horizontal line to the right and left of the center as shown in Fig. 3-11. The line to the right of center will mark the location for the 3 and the line to the left will mark the location for the 9. Starting from the far right side of the protractor, read up until you find the 30° mark. This will be where the hour mark

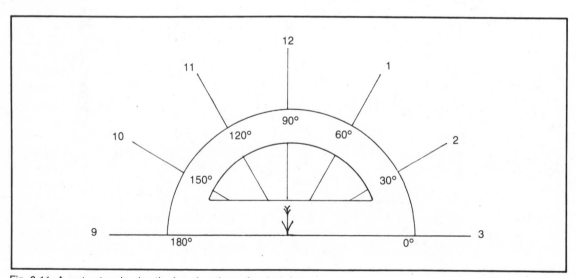

Fig. 3-11. A protractor showing the hour locations of a clock face.

for the 2 is found. Continue up the protractor making a mark at the 60° and 90° points for the 1 and 12 hour marks respectively. From the 90° mark, start down the left side of the protractor, making a mark at the 120° and 150° points. This locates the hour marks of 11 and 10. What you should have now is a board with the center hole location and the top half of the clock face laid out. To find the location of hours 4, 5, 6, 7, and 8, turn the protractor upside down and repeat these steps.

How far from the center are the hour marks to be? This can only be decided by the craftsman. If hands have been purchased, the distance can be determined from the length of the minute hand. For example, if the minute hand from center to the tip is 4 inches long, then it is necessary to measure on the clock face 4 inches from the center hole to each of

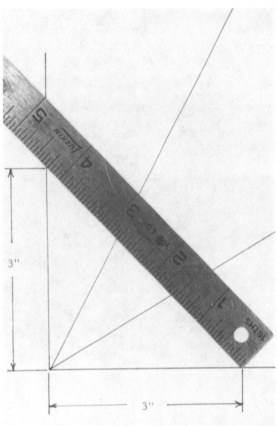

Fig. 3-13. Measurement method to lay out a clock face.

the marks made with the protractor (Fig. 3-12). This will assure that each hour marker is the same distance from the center. You can also use a compass. Set it for the same distance as the length of the minute hand and draw an arc around the clock face center. Where this arc crosses, the protractor marks will be the location of the hour markers.

Another way to find the hour marks is by the measurement method (Fig. 3-13). This does not require any investment in equipment other than the ruler or tape measure (which you probably already have). Nevertheless, this method does not produce clock faces with the same amount of accuracy as the protractor method. Again, begin by finding the center hole. From this point, draw a horizontal line to the right for 3 inches and a vertical line straight up from the center hole (3 inches). Laying the ruler

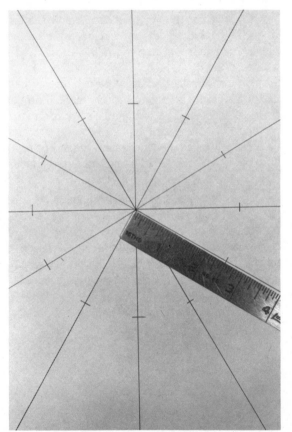

Fig. 3-12. Determining the distance from center to hour markers.

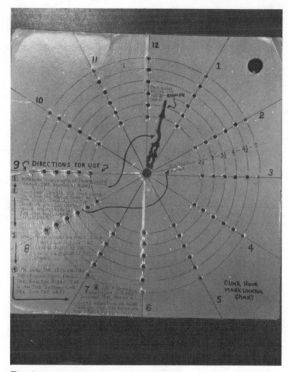

Fig. 3-14. A clock hour location chart.

distance from the center.

MAKING A CLOCK HOUR-MARK LOCATOR CHART

If you intend to mass produce clocks either as a hobby, for gifts, or for resale, it will save time to make a clock hour-mark locator chart (Fig. 3-14).

The chart should be made of a heavy piece of cardboard such as poster board. Begin by cutting out a piece 12 inches square. Find the center and layout lines extended from the center hole through the hour marks. Locate the hour markers by either of the two methods described earlier in this chapter. Using a compass, draw circles with radii of 2 ½ inches, 3 inches, 3½ inches, 4 inches, 4½ inches, and 5 inches. Wherever the circles touch the hour mark lines, draw a 3/16-inch hole. Also drill a ⅜-inch hole in the center. Then follow these simple directions for use:

☐ Measure the length of the minute hand.

☐ Find that length, or one close to it, on the radius chart. This will be the radius used for the hour markers.

☐ Lay the chart on the clock face. Be sure to line up the center hole of the chart with the center of the clock face. Also be sure the 12 mark is directly on top.

☐ Using a sharp pencil or sharp-pointed tool, make a slight mark or indention through the holes along the radius line.

When building several clocks, finding the positions of the hour markers is always one of the most time-consuming operations. By making one of these easy-to-build hour marker locators, the job of finding the positions will require little time, and the accuracy of the finished product can be assured.

at the end of both of these 3-inch lines, make a mark at the 1 9/16-inch and 2¾-inch marks. Draw a straight line from the center hole through these two points and you will have the 12-, 1-, 2- and 3-hour marks. To find the others, you will have to repeat these steps for the rest of the clock face.

To assure that each hour marker will be the same distance from the center hole, you must measure the required distance along each of the 12 lines or use a compass to draw a circle, making a mark at each of the 12 lines. These marks will all be an equal

Chapter 4

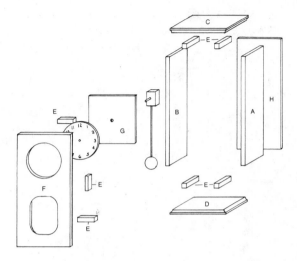

Kitchen Clocks

EVERYONE NEEDS A CLOCK IN THEIR KITCHEN. It is a useful place to have the time ready at hand. The cook uses it when preparing meals, and the rest of the family uses it when running to and through the kitchen. There are many commercially made clocks available. Some are very attractive and others are extremely gaudy. By investing a few dollars and a few hours of leisure time, you can create distinctive kitchen clocks.

In this chapter there are instructions for four different types of kitchen clocks. The apple clock is made of wood and is in the shape of an apple. The pot- and pan-clock is rather unusual. It is created by using discarded cooking pots and pans. The third type is the butcher-block clock. It has a glued wood face in the style of the old butcher's chopping block. Also included in this section is a bread-board design. The bread-board clock is built using the same construction techniques as the butcher-block clock.

You are sure to be proud of whichever clock you decide to build. They are of a popular design and make an item that is profitable to the craftsman who builds for resale.

APPLE CLOCK

The apple clock is an inexpensive, relatively simple clock to build. This clock can be built using hand or power tools. By following the directions, the novice or professional craftsman will be proud to display or sell the finished project (Fig. 4-1).

Select a piece of wood with a thickness of at least 1½ inches. The width and length should be approximately 11¼ inches. A piece of 2- × -2-inch pine (actual measurements of 1½ inches by 11¼ inches) will work fine. Other types of wood with more pleasing grain patterns might be more to your liking. See Table 4-1.

After the wood has been cut to the length and you have a piece measuring the necessary size, locate the center of the board. It is much easier to locate the center now while the board is square rather than after it has been cut to shape.

Find the center by using a straightedge to draw two diagonal lines connecting opposite corners as in Fig. 4-2. The center is where the two lines meet. Drill a small hole or drive a thin nail through the

Fig. 4-1. Apple clock.

easily be broken off. Trace around the paper templet.

The next step is to cut out the shape of the apple using a coping saw or a power saw (if one is available). Cut away the waste wood around the entire apple shape, but leave some stock in the area of the stem. This should be left uncut while the shaping and other operations are being done so as to protect it from breaking.

When using a coping saw, remember to cut slightly outside the line. Then file down to the line. This allows you to file away any saw marks without changing the size or the design.

Turn the wood over to the back side and lay out the size and shape of the recess that must be cut in the wood to allow for the clock movement (Fig.

wood. Remove the nail (leaving a hole). The hole will remain in the wood to mark the center point. Pencil marks seem to find a way of disappearing.

You should now draw out the apple design. The easiest way to do this is to draw out a 1-inch grid pattern on a large sheet of paper (see Fig. 4-3). Then sketch out the apple design on the grid pattern. Be sure to also mark the center hole on the sketch.

Cut out this paper templet and lay it on the 11-¼-×-11¼-inch board; be sure to align the center mark on the paper with the center mark on the board. Also make sure the grain of the wood is running up and down. Otherwise the apple stem can

Fig. 4-2. Determining the location of the hand-shaft hole of the apple clock.

Table 4-1. Apple Clock Materials.

Quantity	Size	Description
1	1½″ × 11¼″ × 11¼″	clock body
1	hand-shaft to fit ⅝″ thick dial	battery clock movement
1		set of hands to fit movement
1		set of hour markers

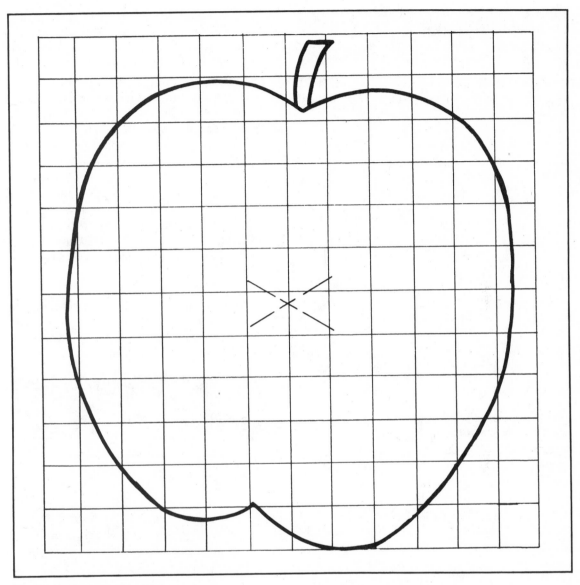

Fig. 4-3. Apple clock grid pattern.

4-4). The size of this recess is determined by the size of your movement. Because each is different, it is impossible to give actual dimensions.

Most clock movements have a hand-shaft length that will allow for a ¼-inch-thick dial. Because ¼ of an inch is very thin, it is advisable that a long hand-shaft be used. The long hand-shaft length will allow for a dial thickness of up to ⅝ of an inch.

Using a chisel and mallet, carefully remove the wood from within the area; take care not to penetrate through the front side. Once you have chiseled the recess down to within ⅝ of an inch of the front side, drill the hole that the hand-shaft will fit through. Usually this is a ⅜-inch hole, but check the size of your clock movement to make certain. Drill from the front of the wood to prevent chipping the face.

What you should have at this point is a piece of

Fig. 4-4. Clock movement recess of the apple clock.

Sanding—no matter how boring and monotonous—is a must. Start sanding with medium paper, 80- or 100-grit, to remove any large scratches or other imperfections. Then progress to a finer, 120- to 180-grit paper. This will give a smooth surface. Always sand with the grain not across it (Fig. 4-5).

The clock can be finished in any of the normal methods. Depending on the type of wood used, you might want to use a stain and varnish or an oil finish. Possibly you will want to paint the clock to match or contrast the decor of the room in which it will be hung. No matter which method is chosen for the clock, it is important to read and follow the manufacturer's instructions when you use a product.

The only thing left now is to find the location for the hour markers and apply the markers to the face. Instructions for both of these procedures can be found in Chapter 3.

If you have followed these instructions, you now have a clock of which you can be proud. Remember, with the more experience you gain each project becomes easier and will take less time to

wood cut in the shape of an apple, with a thick stem, and a ⅜-inch hole drilled through the center. On the back side there should be a recessed hole large enough to fit the clock movement. Move on to the next operation, shaping and rounding the sides of the apple. This shaping operation can be done with files, knives, or Stanley Surform tools. Rounding the corner between the side and front surface is done to give a more realistic appearance to the apple.

Being careful not to break off the stem, cut around it according to your design. Because this will always be a weak spot in the project, take care to protect the stem. In the event it does break off, do not throw the whole thing away in disgust. Glue it back on using a quality wood glue.

Now it is time to prepare the surface of the clock for its final finish. Remember that the finish can only be as good as the surface on which applied. The preparation of the surface is very important, and time must be taken to ensure a good job.

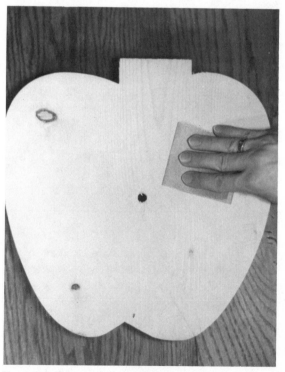

Fig. 4-5. Sand only with the grain of the wood.

complete. If you are not satisfied with the result of the clock, do not become discouraged. Try again!

POT-AND-PAN CLOCKS

This section describes the construction of a kitchen clock made of old pots and pans. Even though most of the other projects in this book are made of wood, this is an example of using another material as a medium for the craftsman. Some craftsmen might consider this project a bit off the wall, but if it is made correctly and with taste, this low-cost clock could become a fast selling item or a project friends will beg you to make for them.

The key part of this clock is the type of pot used. Unless price is of no concern, the use of new pots is out. That leaves the task of finding old pots, and it might be more difficult than you think. After all, if a pot is in bad enough shape to be disposed of, then chances are it is not in any condition to use as a

Fig. 4-7. Drill a pilot hole through a cast-iron frying pan, and then a hand-shaft hole.

clock. A source for the pot is a problem, but the following are some suggestions that might be of assistance in locating them. Free sources might be friends and relatives. Possibly they have some pots stashed in the attic or garage. Put the word out that you are looking for assorted pots and pans and you will be surprised at the goods or tips you will receive.

After this free source of material is exhausted, next look for old pots or pans that can be purchased at low prices. Flea markets, garage sales, yard sales, or estate sales will most likely be the best places to look. Pots and pans are not big sellers at these types of sales, so you should be able to haggle about the price. While at these sales, be alert for anything else you should use in clockmaking. An-

Fig. 4-6. A pot-and-pan clock.

tique stores, while they may be more expensive, might sell old pots or pans with "character" that will make distinct kitchen clocks.

The only problem you might encounter during the construction of this clock is locating and drilling the center hole. It might be hard to find the exact center because pots and pans generally are rounded where the bottom meets the sides. Finding an approximate center will be all that is needed, but be as accurate with your approximation as possible.

When you find the center, mark it by making an indentation in the metal with a center punch or large nail. The indentation will help to keep the drill bit on the center when drilling. It is important that all layout work is done on the bottom of the pan—not the inside. Also, be sure to drill from the bottom into the pan. Drilling from the bottom in will give you a smooth surface around the hole while the inside will be jagged. Light filing will remove this jagged edge so it won't interfere with the clock movement.

The type of pan you use does not really matter as long as its condition is not too bad and it is deep enough for the clock movement. An iron fry pan will make an attractive clock; but if you intend to drill the hole for the hand-shaft with a hand drill, be prepared for a long, slow-moving process. Nevertheless, many are made of cast iron (which is somewhat easier to drill). Even if you use a power drill, the drill bit must be very sharp. Drilling a hole the size needed for most hand-shafts (usually ⅜ of an inch) can be made easier if you first drill a pilot hole (Fig. 4-7). This is a small hole approximately ⅛ of an inch in diameter drilled in the center. This hole guides the larger drill and makes it easier cutting because some material is already removed.

Copper-bottom pans can also be used. If the bottom doesn't clean up to a spotless finish, don't worry. The stains might add to the appearance of the pot clock.

The type of hour markers used on this clock should be determined by the finish on the pan bottom. Bright brass-colored markers and hands would be a pleasing contrast to a black, iron frying pan. Black numerals or markers and black hands would look best on a copper-bottom or chrome pan.

Find the location of the hour markers using one of the methods described in Chapter 3. Mark them with a center punch. The method for applying hour markers will be different (depending on the type of marker used). If you need an adhesive to apply the markers, one of the epoxy adhesives will be best for gluing them to the metal.

If the pot or pan has a ring at the end of the handle, this will be all that is necessary for hanging the clock. When there is no ring and the pan is not too deep, the hanger molded into most plastic cases of the battery movement will work fine. The problem begins when neither of these methods will work. The easiest way to hang this type of pan will be to glue a block of wood to the inside top of the pan and use this for hanging purposes (Fig. 4-8).

The type of pot you use determines the type of finish you should apply. Several pots and pans can be left natural. For example, the iron fry pan that

Fig. 4-8. Alternate method to wall hanging.

has been used for years and shows its age by rust and other distress marks will look best if it is left as it is. The copper-bottom pans can be left natural or, if the bottom is too stained, could be repainted with copper spray paint. For that matter, the whole pan can be painted a color that will match or contrast the colors used in the kitchen.

If you decide to leave the copper bottom as the color you want, a coat of varnish will help keep the copper from tarnishing and also protect it from scratches. Whatever finish you use, I am sure you will find that this project shows pleasing results with a small investment of time.

BUTCHER-BLOCK CLOCK

Any type of wood can be used to build a butcher-block clock (Fig. 4-9). If hardwood such as maple is used, it will more closely resemble the butcher's chopping block. The wood is used with the edge grain showing rather than the surface grain. The old butcher chopping blocks were made this way because the edge and end grain are stronger and more resistant to abrasion than the surface. Hence the name butcher-block clock.

Fig. 4-9. A butcher-block clock.

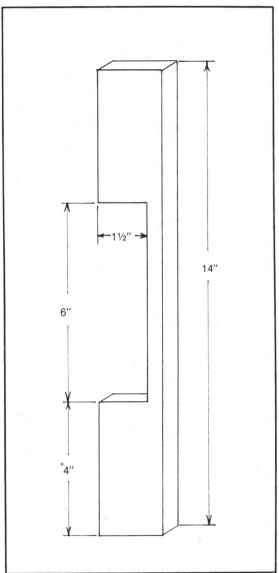
Fig. 4-10. Layout for the butcher-block clock movement cavity.

Table 4-2. Basic Butcher-Block Clock Materials.

Quantity	Size	Description
16	¾″ × 2″ × 14″	clock body
1	⅝″ or longer hand-shaft	battery clock movement
1		set of hands to fit movement
1		set of hour markers (optional)

35

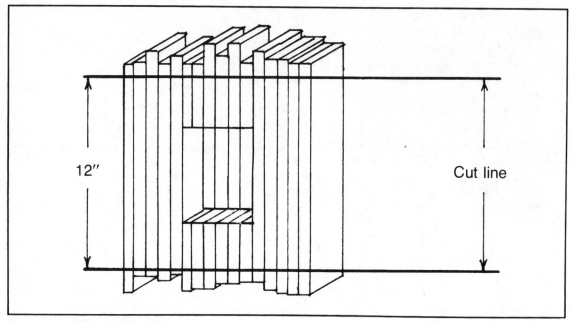

Fig. 4-11. Squaring off the ends of the butcher-block clock.

In this example, ¾-inch wood is used, but actually any thickness can be used. You will need 16 pieces of ¾-inch stock measuring 2 inches wide and 14 inches long. On six of these boards, it is necessary to make a cutout in which the movement will fit. See Table 4-2 and 4-3. Measure 4 inches up from the bottom of the board, make a mark, measure 6 inches above this mark, and again mark the board (Fig. 4-10). This indicates the length of the opening. Repeat this on each of the six boards. Measure 1½ inches in on the boards at the points you have just marked.

Lay out the pattern on the board as it is shown in Fig. 4-10. Using a coping saw, followed by a file,

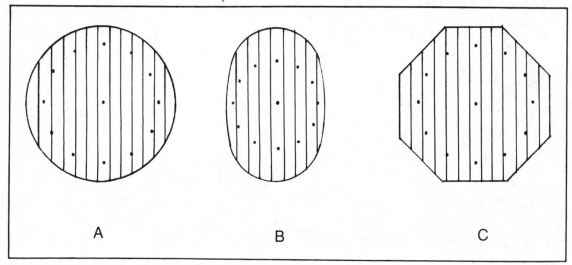

Fig. 4-12. Alternate butcher-block clock designs: (A) round, (B) oval, (C) octagon.

Fig. 4-13. A butcher-block clock made of alternating, contrasting color woods.

Table 4-3. Bread-Board Clock Materials.

Quantity	Size	Description
10	¾″ × 2″ × 14″	clock body
1	long hand-shaft	battery movement
1	2¼″ to 2¾″	set of hands
1		set of hour markers

Gluing the boards together into the solid block is done next. Using a quality wood glue, coat both surfaces of the wood—starting with the five outside pieces—then coat the six cutout pieces, and finally coat the other five outside pieces. Make sure when these pieces are clamped together that the six inside pieces line up at the cutout. If the ends aren't lined up exactly, don't worry because some will later be removed. Allow this to dry thoroughly before any more work is done. Consult the directions for the glue to learn its drying time.

Using a square, draw a line at a right angle to the side near the bottom of the glued board (Fig. 4-11). Working from the front side of the clock, cut along this line squaring it to the side. Measure 12 inches up, draw another line, and cut again at this point. The board should now measure 2 × 12 × 12 inches. File and sand the cut ends as needed. If any of the 16 boards are not exactly level with the rest, use a plane to level the surface of the clock. Lightly draw a line across the surface from one corner diagonally to the opposite corner. Repeat this using the other corners. Where these two lines meet is the center of the board. This is where the hole for the movement hand-shaft will be drilled.

remove the ¾-×1½-×-6-inch piece. Because you will be leaving a thickness of only ½ of an inch, be careful not to cut too deep. If the movement intended for use will not fit in the suggested cutout, it will be necessary to either enlarge the 6-inch opening or to cut out the opening in more than six boards. Six boards will give an opening with a width of 4½ inches. This opening could be chiseled out, but if a hardwood is used chiseling would be a lengthy ordeal.

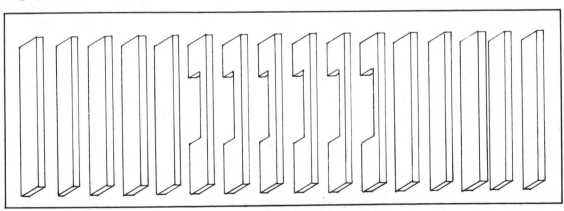

Fig. 4-14. An exploded view of the butcher-block clock showing the wood parts.

Fig. 4-15. A bread-board clock built similar to the butcher-block clock, but with a bread-board design.

After the block is cut to the correct size, the surface is planed flat, and the center hole is drilled, the next operation is sanding the surface. Be careful to only sand in the direction of the grain. Never sand across the grain! Sand using progressively finer grit paper until you get the smoothness you prefer.

At this point, the only work that remains is to finish the surface in a manner you choose, apply the hour markers, and install the clock movement. Each of these operations are covered in detail in other chapters.

The butcher-block clock described in this section is the traditional square shape. It is not necessary to limit yourself to this shape alone. There are many designs that can be created. An interesting deviation from tradition that can be simply made is to cut the clock into a round, oval, or octagon shape (A, B, and C of Fig. 4-12). These three designs don't require any construction techniques different from the basic butcher-block clock, other than cutting it into the desired shape.

Another interesting variation—requiring no more work than the traditional style, is made of two or more different types of wood. Maple or pine are light-colored woods with an attractive grain pattern; mahogany or walnut will contrast them with its dark tone. If these light and dark colors are glued together alternately, the contrast produces a distinctive and attractive clock (Fig. 4-13). See also Fig. 4-14.

The type of hour marker you choose to use can drastically alter the appearance of the basic butcher-block clock. By drilling ½-inch or ⅝-inch holes completely through the clock at the 12, 3, 6, and 9 hour marks—and ⅜-inch holes at the other marks—you can create a clock that shares the butcher-block material of the past with the methods and appearance of today.

These are only a few possible alternates to the basic butcher-block clock. Use one of them, a combination of them, or all of them to create a truly distinctive, attractive clock. See Fig. 4-15.

Chapter 5

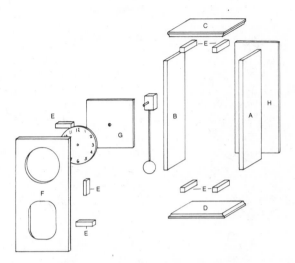

Mantel Clocks

IN EARLY AMERICA, HOMES WERE HEATED BY the warmth produced by a fireplace. The fireplace was usually built in a central location that became the gathering point for the family. The outgrowth of this was a need for a clock that would meet the family's needs and also complement the style of the room. The mantel clock, a clock small enough to fit on the fireplace mantel, was the obvious answer.

The mantel size dictated that the cabinet must be small. Therefore, it was necessary to use small, spring-driven movements. There was no room for weight shells to drop, and obviously electric or battery movements were not used at that time.

THE BROOKFIELD

The Brookfield (Fig. 5-1) is easily made using hand tools and requires only a short time to complete. Despite its ease of construction, the result looks like a high-priced reproduction of an expensive antique.

The body of the clock is made up of seven separate pieces of wood, each having the same outside dimensions. The inside treatment each piece receives varies slightly. The first piece (part A of Fig. 5-2) is cut from a board ¼-inch thick, 6 inches wide, and 12⅛ inches long. The height of the clock might have to be shortened or lengthened depending on the length of the pendulum you use. The 12⅛-inch size cabinet is designed to be used with a pendulum length of 8 1/16 inches. Pendulum length is measured from the center of the hand-shaft of the movement to the bottom of the bob. Square the bottom end of this board to ensure that it will sit level when it is attached to the base. Measure 9½ inches up from the bottom and 3 inches in from the sides (Fig. 5-3). This will be the location of the hand-shaft hole. It is also the center point for drawing the curved top.

Do not drill the center hole until you have drawn the curved top. Using a compass, set the opening for 3 inches and lightly push the point of the compass into the wood where the hand-shaft hole will be drilled. Draw the arc with the compass from

Fig. 5-1. Brookfield clock.

one side of the board to the other. Cut out the arc using a coping saw and file to shape the curved top.

If your movement has a pendulum, you should cut out the pendulum window. Any shape—such as rectangular, star, half-moon, circle, elipse, your initials, or almost anything else that will fit in the space allowed—can be cut. The exact location and size of the window should be determined by the length of the pendulum and the distance the bob swings from the center to the sides. Clock suppliers give this information in their catalogs.

Once the first piece is cut out, you will be able to use it as a templet for laying out the rest of the pieces. Trace the outside shape on the remaining six boards. Cut them out and shape them as was done on the first piece.

The four pieces (part B in Fig. 5-2) that make up the bulk of the clock case, found between the

¼-inch front and the solid back, are all made alike; each measures ¾ × 6 × 12⅛ inches. Measure in 1 inch on all sides as shown in Fig. 5-4. Starting from the bottom, cut with a coping saw along the lines just drawn. Remove the inside portion. Repeat these steps for all five of the inside pieces. The area formed by the cutout will be the clock movement and pendulum cavity. If this does not provide enough room for your movement, there will have to be an alteration to the dimensions.

The first five pieces of the clock body are now roughly shaped and ready to be assembled. Using a quality wood glue, apply one coat to the four ¾-inch inside pieces (parts B) and the one ¼-inch front piece (part A). Be careful to line them up as closely as possible at this point. It will save time and work later. Clamp and set this assembly aside to dry (Fig. 5-5). Begin work on the ¾-inch clock case back (part C).

Part C, the back, will not have any cutouts, but four holes will be drilled in it to attach it to the clock body with screws. Drill two ⅛-inch holes ½ of an inch in from the edges and 1 inch up from the bottom. Drill two more holes ½ inch in from the edge and 7 inches up from the bottom (Fig. 5-6). These holes are for the screws that will hold the back to the rest of the clock body. It is not glued on because removing the back provides easy access to the clock movement. When the glued portion of the clock body has had sufficient time to dry, attach the back using four 1½-inch number-six wood screws.

Using a file or another forming tool on the

Table 5-1. Brookfield Clock Materials.

Part	Quantity	Size	Description
A	1	¼″ × 6″ × 12⅛″	front
B	4	¾″ × 6″ × 12⅛″	interior parts of body
C	1	¾″ × 6″ × 12⅛″	back
D	1	¾″ × 5¾″ × 7½″	base
	4	1½″, number six	flathead wood screws
	4	1¼″, number six	flathead wood screws
	1	5″ to 6″ diameter	dial and bezel
	1	8″ pendulum length	clock movement
	1		set of hands to fit movement

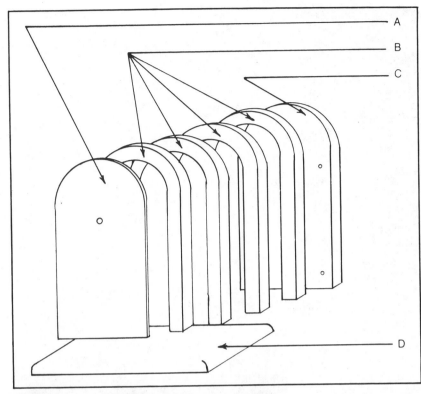

A

B

C

D

Fig. 5-2. Exploded view of the Brookfield clock showing its seven wood component parts (dial and movement used in this sample are courtesy of Klockit).

3″ R

9½″

Fig. 5-3. Locating the center on the Brookfield with a compass.

market, finish shaping the round top of the clock body. Do this with the back attached so that all six parts will be shaped at the same time. *Important*: File the rounded part from the bottom of the clock body toward the top of the rounded part (Fig. 5-7). If you file in the other direction, you run the risk of splintering the wood on the sides. Starting with a medium-grade sandpaper and working progressively down to a very fine paper, sand the rounded surface of the clock cabinet until it is smooth and free from file marks and scratches.

The base of the clock is the only piece remaining to be made. This is constructed of the same type of wood as the rest of the clock. Cut the piece to ¾ × 5 ¾ × 7 ½ inches. Make sure it is square at each corner.

Using a plane, wood rasp, file, whittling knife, or router, round the upper corner of the base on three sides only (Fig. 5-8). Rough shape these corners with one of the above-mentioned tools and finish the rounding process with decreasing grades of sandpaper.

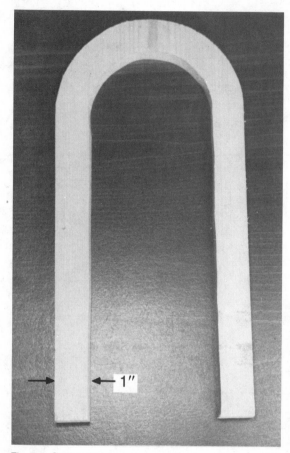

Fig. 5-4. Cutting the clock movement and pendulum cavity.

bezel to the ¼-inch clock front according to the manufacturer's instructions. If the opening described in the instructions is too small for the clock mechanism, it can be expanded. If more space is needed, you will have to expand the outside dimensions of the clock body.

You will soon find that you have created a clock that is a work of art. After building the first clock, the builder will be surprised how fast he can build others like it. This clock easily lends itself to mass-production techniques. The ease of construction and the beauty of the results make this clock one that is a welcome gift or a profitable resale item.

AUTOMOBILE CLOCK

The auto clock (Fig. 5-11) is not the normal mantel

On the bottom of the base, you must locate the positions for the screws that will hold the base to the body of the clock. Refer to Fig. 5-9 for layout details. Drill two holes 2¼ inches in from either side. The first will be 2 inches back from the front edge. The next two will be 1¼ inches from the back edge. At these four points, drill a 3/16-inch hole to act as a pilot hole for the screw. Now form a countersink using a countersink bit (Fig. 5-10). If you do not have one, you can use a drill bit of a larger size. This is a recess drilled at each of the three pilot holes so the head of the screw will be below the wood surface. Use three 1¼-inch number-six wood screws to attach the base to the body.

Once the clock has been assembled and all sanding has been done, apply the type of finish, stain, varnish, etc., that you prefer. Install the

Fig. 5-5. Clamping parts A and the four parts B together.

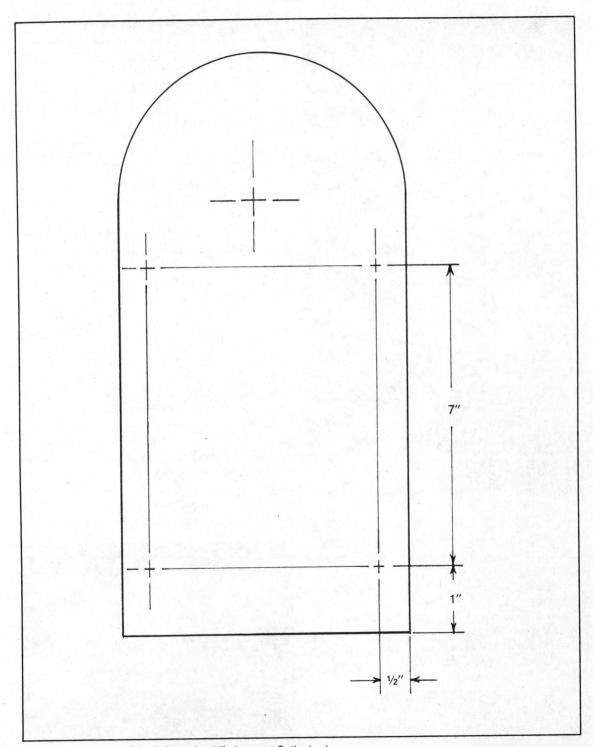

Fig. 5-6. The location of the holes to be drilled on part C, the back.

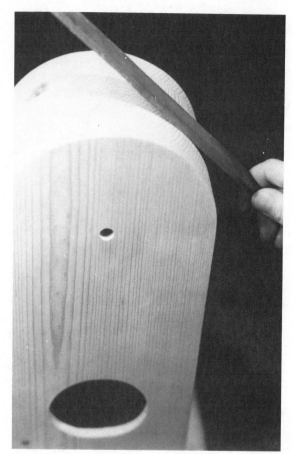

Fig. 5-7. Shaping the curved top of the Brookfield.

Table 5-2. Automobile Clock Materials.

Part	Quantity	Size	Description
A	1	¼" × 6" × 10"	face
B	4	¾" × 6" × 10"	interior parts
C	2	⅝" × 1½" × 10"	fenders
	4	1¾" diameter	wheels: wood, plastic, or rubber
	4	to fit wheel axle holes	screws
	1		battery clock movement
	1		set of hour markers

ment cavity. Measure in from the left side 4 inches, and then another 3 inches from that spot (Fig. 5-12). From the bottom, measure up 1 ¾ inches and ¾ of an inch down from the top. This is the location of the movement cavity. Using a coping saw or a power saw, cut the movement cavity area out of the four ¾-inch thick pieces. An entrance cut can be made from the bottom.

Glue the four ¾-inch pieces together; be sure to line up the movement cavity area (Fig. 5-13). Also, glue the ¼-inch thick front piece to the block containing the movement cavity. Set this assembly aside to thoroughly dry before anything more is done to it.

The next phase of construction can be done while the other piece is drying. Using the grid pattern shown in Fig. 5-14, draw the shape of the car on heavy paper or cardboard. Cut out the paper templet and trace it onto the front of the wood block.

When the glued block is dry, cut out along the traced outline of the car. The best saw to use for

clock found on the mantels and desks of America. This is an original and unusual clock that will capture the love of all. It is easy to make with only five pieces of wood and four wooden, plastic, or rubber wheels. It should also be a fun project to do with children.

The wood used in the auto clock can be of any type, as long as it is of the correct thickness, width, and length. Select a piece of wood ¼ × 6 × 10 inches. This will serve as the side of the clock (part A). It must be ¼ of an inch thick so that the clock movement hand-shaft will fit through. See Table 5-2.

Now choose four pieces of wood with the same length and width as the ¼-inch thick piece, but ¾ of an inch thick (parts B). On these four ¾-inch pieces, it is necessary to draw and cut out the clock move-

Fig. 5-8. Shaping the edge and two ends of the base, part D.

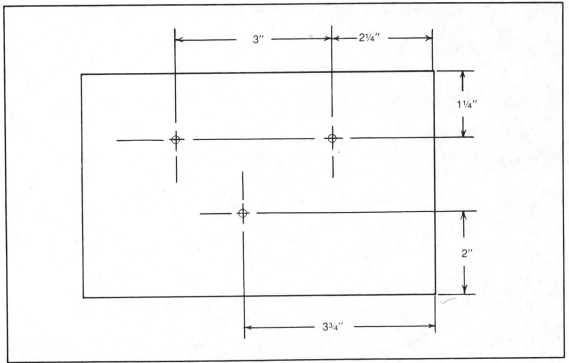

Fig. 5-9. The location of the mounting holes in the clock base.

this is a bandsaw. With patience and care, however, this job can be completed with a coping saw. The shape of the car has been kept as simple as possible to ease in the cutting.

After the cutting operation has been completed, it is necessary to file the rough edges and smooth out any imperfections that might have occurred during cutting. Use various grades of sandpaper to thoroughly sand the edges and front surface.

The fenders are the next to be built. Use the grid pattern shown in Fig. 5-15 to make a templet. Trace the templet onto part C (the two ⅝-inch thick, 1½ inches wide, and 10 inches long pieces of wood). Cut these out and again file and sand them smooth. It is much easier to sand them now rather than trying to sand it when it is glued to the body.

Locate the center of the clock-movement cavity, where the hand-shaft will extend through the ¼-inch front.

Determine the diameter of the movement hand-shaft, usually ⅜ inch, and drill a hole through the ¼-inch thick front. It would be a good idea to trial fit the movement into the clock by setting it up completely with the hands and a battery. If the

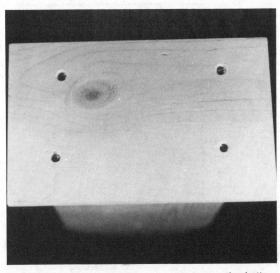

Fig. 5-10. Countersinking the screw holes on the bottom surface of part D, the base.

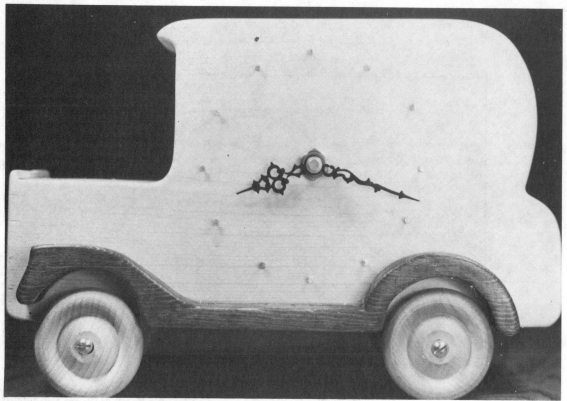

Fig. 5-11. The beginning of an automobile clock.

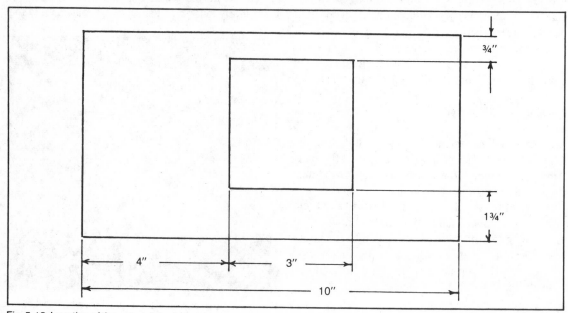

Fig. 5-12. Location of the automobile clock movement cavity.

Fig. 5-13. Clamping of parts A and B of the automobile clock.

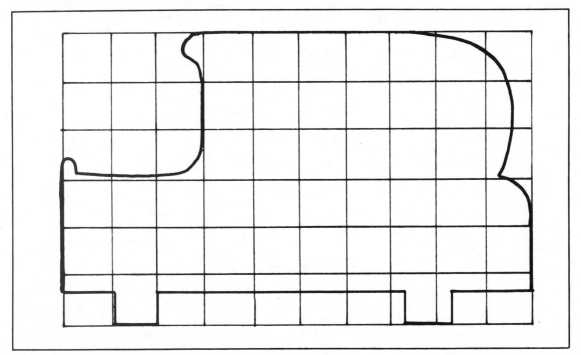

Fig. 5-14. Automobile clock grid pattern; each square equals 1 inch.

Fig. 5-15. Grid pattern for the automobile clock fenders; each square equals 1 inch.

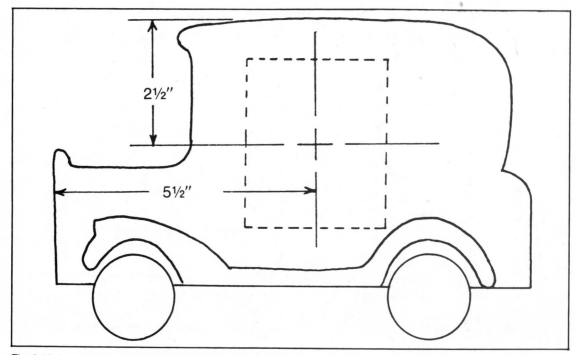

2½″

5½″

Fig. 5-16. Locating the hand-shaft hole for the automobile clock.

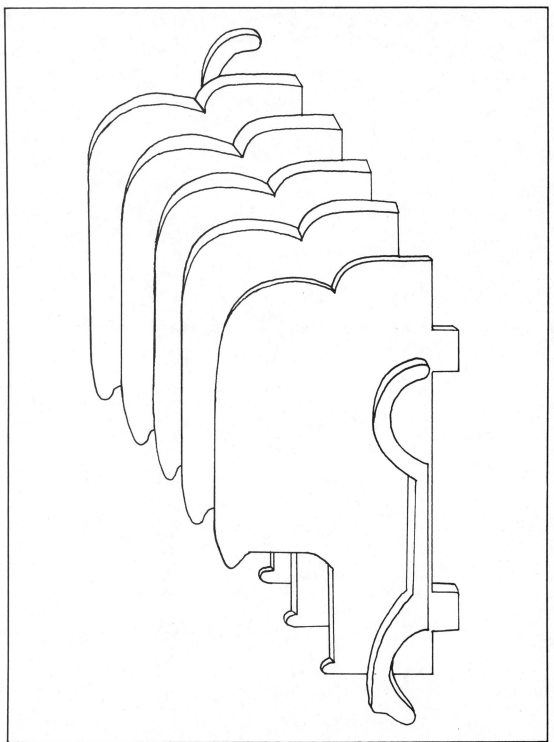

Fig. 5-17. Exploded view of the automobile clock showing the wood parts (dial and movement used in this sample are courtesy of Klockit).

Fig. 5-18. A traditional mantel clock.

hand-shaft hole is not large enough or the movement does not fit in the cavity, corrective measures can be taken before the final sanding and finishing. See Fig. 5-17.

There are four ways to obtain the wheels for the automobile clock. The first is to cut a 1¾-inch-diameter circle out of ½-inch-thick wood. Locate the center, drill a hole, and attach the wheels to the body with roundhead wood screws. Another possibility is to find rubber, plastic, or wooden wheels on broken or discarded toys. (If you have children, you are bound to have some broken toys.) Hobby shops are another source for wheels. Most hobby shops sell rubber wheels in many sizes for use on airplane models. These wheels look nice on the clock, but they are more expensive.

If you prefer to make the entire project of wood and want the project to have a professional appearance, commercially made wooden wheels in a variety of sizes are available. A supplier for wooden wheels can be found in most woodworking magazines.

Finally, you need to finish your clock using paint, stain, or varnish. No matter what finish or type of wheels you prefer to use, the clock will add a bit of originality to any room.

TRADITIONAL MANTEL CLOCK

The mantel clock (Fig. 5-18) has been a long-standing favorite of American clock admirers. Its classic, gentle curves combined with a commercially produced dial and bezel make a beautiful addition to any room.

Table 5-3. Traditional Mantel Clock Materials.

Part	Quantity	Size	Description
A	1	¼″ × 8″ × 17″	front
B	4	¾″ × 8″ × 17″	cabinet body
C	1	¾″ × 8″ × 17″	cabinet back
	1	approximately 5″ diameter	dial and bezel setup
	4	brass brads	for dial
	3	1½″, number 8 flathead	wood screws
	1		clock movement
	1		set of hands to fit movement

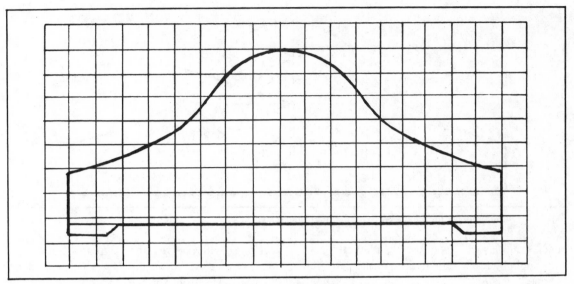

Fig. 5-19. The traditional mantel clock grid pattern. Each square equals 1 inch.

This clock is made in a manner similar to the Brookfield clock because it has several pieces of wood glued to form the body. It has a ¼-inch thick front, with five ¾-inch boards making up the remainder of the clock case. See Table 5-3.

Begin building this clock by selecting a ¼-inch thick piece of wood (part A). This will be the front of the clock so choose a board that has a pleasing grain pattern. The ¼-inch thick board and the five ¾-inch

thick pieces should measure at least 8 inches wide and 17 inches long. These will form the body of the clock and will also contain the clock movement cavity.

Using the grid method shown in Fig. 5-19, develop a pattern for the clock cabinet. It is best to first draw it out on cardboard or heavy paper and then trace it onto the six pieces of wood. It can be drawn directly on the wood, but this leaves the

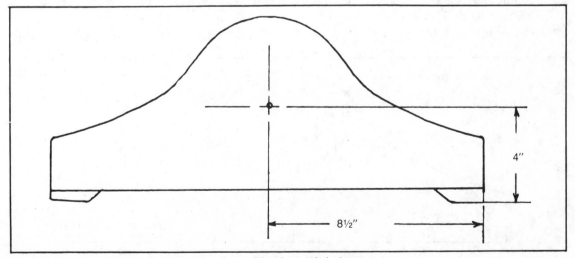

Fig. 5-20. Location of the hand-shaft hole on the traditional mantel clock.

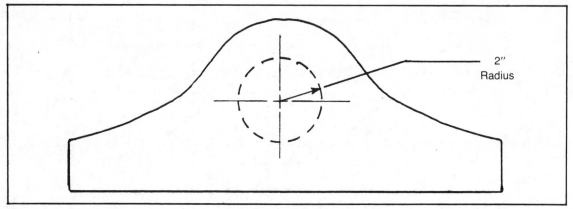

Fig. 5-21. Drawing out the movement cavity of the traditional mantel clock.

pencil grid that will need to be sanded off.

Begin by tracing the outline of the pattern on the one ¼-inch thick board, (part A) and also on the five ¾-inch boards (parts B). On each section, mark the center hole location for the hand-shaft of the clock movement. This point can be located by measuring over 8½ inches from the end and up 4 inches from the bottom (Fig. 5-20).

After tracing the templet onto each of the seven boards, use a coping saw or power saw to cut them out. Be careful not to cut inside the line. It is better to cut 1/16 of an inch outside the line and file down to the line. There is no need to do any sanding at this point. Wait until the seven sections are assembled and then file and sand at the same time.

Until now the sections have all been alike (with the exception of the one that is ¼-inch thick). Now

each piece will receive a special treatment that will allow it to perform the function for which it has been designed. The front (part A) is the easiest of the parts to make. All it requires is a hole ⅜ inch in diameter drilled at the center hole location.

Four of the ¾-inch sections are all treated alike. Set a compass for a 2-inch radius and draw a circle using the center hole location for the center of the circle (Fig. 5-21). These four-inch diameter circles will later be cut out to form the clock movement cavity. If a four-inch diameter cavity is not large enough for the clock movement, increase the size. If a clock cavity larger than six inches in diameter is required, the height and length of the entire clock cabinet will need to be increased.

If the movement cavity is not deep enough, it will be necessary to increase the size by adding one

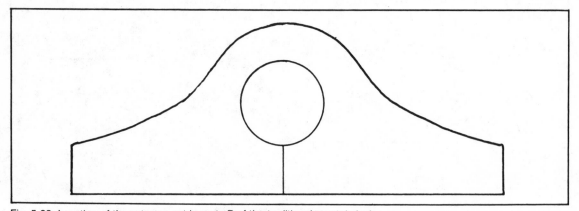

Fig. 5-22. Location of the entrance cut in parts B of the traditional mantel clock.

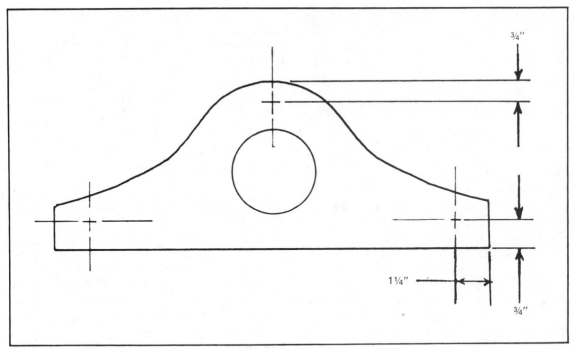

Fig. 5-23. Location of the screw holes on the clock cabinet back, part C.

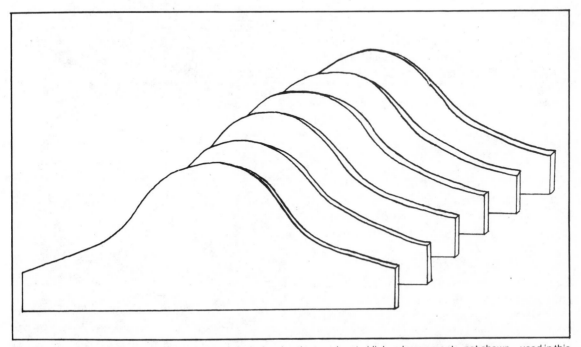

Fig. 5-24. Exploded view of the traditional mantel clock showing the wood parts (dial and movement—not shown—used in this sample are courtesy of Klockit).

or more ¾-inch thick center sections, the B parts.

Begin cutting out the circles with a coping saw. It will be necessary to start the cut on the bottom of the board. If the entrance cut is made anywhere else, it will show on the finished product (Fig. 5-22). Make this cut on only 5 of the ¾-inch thick pieces. The last ¾-inch thick piece does not require a hole.

The first four pieces of the clock have now been roughly shaped and are ready to be assembled. Using a quality wood glue, apply a coat to three ¾-inch inside parts and the one ¼-inch front. Be careful to line them up as close as possible now so that it will save time and work later. Set this assembly aside to dry and begin work on the ¾-inch-thick clock back (part C).

The last piece does not have cutouts, but three holes will be drilled and countersunk in it to attach it to the clock body. These holes will serve as pilot holes for the mounting screws. The first and second holes are located 1 inch from the bottom and 1¼ inches in from the ends. The third hole is found 8½ inches from the end and ¾ of an inch down from the top (Fig. 5-23).

When the main part of the clock has dried, screw the back on using three 1½-inch number-eight flathead wood screws. The clock case is now ready for final shaping. Shape it with files and smooth it with grits of sandpaper.

After the final shaping and sanding has been completed, all that remains to do is to install the clock movement and mount the dial and bezel or whatever face you prefer to use.

As you can tell after making this clock and the Brookfield clock, this method of construction is versatile and can be applied to many other similar projects. See Fig. 5-24. Keep it in mind when you are designing your own clocks and other projects.

PICTURE-FRAME CLOCK

The picture-frame clock (Fig. 5-25) is very unusual and a lot easier to build than it appears. It is easy to make because the decorative front is made by using an unfinished wood picture frame (part A).

Unfinished picture frames can be purchased at most craft stores, frame shops, discount stores, and

Table 5-4. Picture-Frame Clock Materials.

Part	Quantity	Size	Description
A	1	8″ × 10″	picture frame
B	1	8¼″ × 10¼″	glass front to fit frame
C	2	¾″ × 1½″ × ?	cabinet top & bottom
D	2	¾″ × 1½″ × ?	cabinet sides
E	1	⅛″ × ? × ?	masonite cabinet back
	1	6″ diameter	brass dial
	1		battery movement, short shaft
	1		set of hands to fit dial and movement

Note: Dimensions with "?" are variable.

department stores. Frames are available in common sizes such as 4 × 4 inches, 5 × 7 inches, 8 × 11 inches, or 11 × 14 inches. The picture-frame clock can be made with any of these frame sizes, providing there is enough room for the dial and clock movement. Remember that the sizes do not indicate the outside dimensions of the frame, they refer

Fig. 5-25. Picture-frame clock.

to the size of the picture that fits into the frame. See Table 5-4.

If the movement being used has a pendulum, be sure there is enough room for the pendulum to swing from side to side. Also make certain that the pendulum length does not exceed the space available (as measured form the movement hand-shaft to the tip of the pendulum). The minimum size frame that can be used for a pendulum clock is the 11-×-14-inch frame; smaller frames can be used if a pendulum is not used.

If you would like to build this clock, but change the size, it will be necessary for you to do one of two things. First, you could go to a frame shop, give them your size requirements, and have them custom build a frame for you. Compared to the idea of buying an unfinished frame, having one built will be quite expensive. The second option will be for you to build your own frame. This is not hard if you have the proper tools. You will need a miter box, radial-arm saw, or table saw, to cut the 45-degree angles on the corners. You will also need a router, a molder head for the table saw, or a shaper, to create some type of design on the frame front—along with a lot of patience for fitting. The frame will also require that an edge rabbet joint be cut into the back inside edge of the frame. This is where the glass is held into the frame (Fig. 5-26).

If you intend to produce a lot of these clocks for resale, you will want to use the unfinished frame. Its initial cost will be more than building the frame yourself, but it will save a lot of time.

The clock in this example has been built using an unfinished wood frame that holds an 8-×-10-inch picture. Construction begins by obtaining a piece of glass (part B) to fit into the back of the frame. You can cut the glass or buy it from a glass shop. The glass shop is probably the best idea because the clock requires that a hole be drilled through the glass. This is a job best left to a professional with the special glass cutting drill bit (which is tricky to use and expensive to buy). An alternative to the glass is to use clear Plexiglas. This material can be worked with using conventional woodworking tools.

In our example, the hole has been drilled in the

Fig. 5-26. Rear view of a picture frame showing the rabbet cut for the glass to fit into.

center of the glass. To locate this position, place the glass into the frame. Then measure from one end to the other, finding the midpoint. Repeat the process to find the middle from side to side.

Now the woodworking aspect of this project begins. The wood cabinet that fits behind the frame must be built. This cabinet must have the same outside measurements as the outside measurements of the frame being used. Because the unfinished frames are made with the same inside dimensions (8 × 10 in our example) but the frame material can be made at almost any width, the outside size will vary greatly. It is because of this reason that exact sizes for the cabinet are not provided in this section.

The only two sizes that will remain constant are the thickness of the parts, ¾-inch, and the 1 ½-inch width. The top and bottom parts (C) will measure 1½ inches *less* than the outside size of the picture frame. For example, if the frame measures 11 × 13 inches on the outside, the top and bottom

Fig. 5-27. Top and bottom (parts C) of the picture-frame clock case fit between the two sides, parts D. (See Table 5-4.)

parts (C) will have to measure 11 inches, minus 1½ inches, for the thickness of the two ¾-inch sides (parts D, Fig. 5-27), which will be 9½ inches. The length of the sides (D) will remain the same size as the outside of the frame.

To assemble the clock cabinet (Fig. 5-28), glue the sides to the top and bottom. This can be held together with clamps, small finish nails, or 1¼-inch, number-six flathead screws sunk below the surface of the wood. The screw holes can be covered with wood dowels or furniture buttons.

After the clock cabinet has dried, the frame is glued to the cabinet. Before gluing these two parts together, check to make sure the glass can still be put into the frame once the cabinet and frame are joined together. If the glass cannot be inserted, it will be necessary to install the glass in the frame, then glue the frame to the cabinet. This will require extra care while staining and varnishing the assembled cabinet so as not to get the finishing materials on the glass. If this presents a problem, the frame could be hinged to the cabinet.

While gluing the frame to the cabinet, pressure can be applied by laying a board across the frame,

then a weight on top of the board, or clamps can be used.

When dry, the frame and cabinet will require some sanding. It is unusual to find that both pieces fit together exactly. Light sanding will be necessary to make them fit.

Cut a back for the cabinet. This can be made of any thin material. In this case, it is made of ⅛-inch thick Masonite. The size of the back is the same as the outside of the cabinet. The back is held onto the cabinet with four ⅜-inch, number-six panhead screws. The panhead will hold the thin back on without holding the clock too far away from the wall—as roundhead screws will do.

The dial used in the example is 6 inches in diameter, brass, and has an adhesive back so that it can easily be applied to the glass. When applying the dial, be sure the dial hole and the hole in the glass line up perfectly. Also make sure the 12 on the dial is straight up (not to the left or right of the center).

When the dial has been applied and the staining and varnishing (or painting) has been done, it is time to put on the clock back. An interesting effect

56

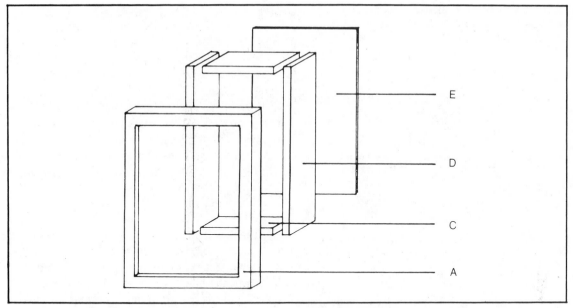

Fig. 5-28. An exploded view showing the parts that make up the picture-frame clock.

that can be obtained is to paint the inside of the cabinet and back panel a flat black. This gives the appearance that the dial is floating in the cabinet. The clock is now completed and ready to hang. It will surely become one of your favorites. You will find it a welcome addition to grace the walls of your home.

BRACKET CLOCK

The bracket clock (Fig. 5-29) is a replica of the early spring-driven clock. The bracket quickly became very popular in Europe, and its popularity poured across the Atlantic to make it a favorite of Americans.

This is not an exact duplicate of the early bracket clock. Modifications in the design have been made to ease in the construction of the clock cabinet. Much of the intricate joint work has been eliminated and replaced by simple butt joints, strengthened by screws and wood supports. All pieces of the clock are rectangular and easily shaped using hand tools. The ease of construction, a handsome and inexpensive dial, and the use of a windup, mechanical, or battery-operated movement creates a clock that the craftsman can be proud

Fig. 5-29. Bracket clock.

Table 5-5. Bracket Clock Materials.

Part	Quantity	Size	Description
A	2	¾" × 4" × 6"	sides
B	2	¾" × 3" × 6"	internal horizontal supports
C	1	¾" × 4¾" × 9"	top
D	1	¾" × 3" × 6"	final
E	1	¾" × 5" × 9½"	base
F	2	¼" × 6" × 6"	plywood back and dial mounting board
	8	½", number four	flathead wood screws
	9	1½", number six	flathead wood screws

to sell or display.

Begin building the clock by first drawing out and cutting the two ¾-×-4-×6-inch sides (parts A). See Table 5-5. It is very important that you square the ends of the wood so they fit properly with the top and the base. Cut two ¾-×-3-×-6-inch internal horizontal supports (parts B). These can be of the same wood as the rest of the clock—or almost any wood in the scrap box—because it will be hidden from view. Make sure the ends of these boards are squared properly because they will be glued between the sides. Glue parts B ¾ of an inch back from the front edge of parts A, ¼ inch in from the back edge, and flush with the top of the two sides (Fig. 5-30). Set this assembly aside to dry.

The top (C), base (E), and final (D), are all made in the same fashion. The only difference is their size. The top is ¾ × 4¾ × 9 inches. The base is ¾ × 5 × 9½ inches. The final is ¾ × 3 × 6 inches. Cut each of these to the correct size; be sure the corners are squared. Use a router, rasp, file, or plane to round the edge on one side and both ends of each of these three pieces (Fig. 5-31). The back edges are not rounded. It will fit flush with the back of the clock body.

Now that all ¾-inch-thick pieces are cut out and shaped, each piece should be sanded until any scratches and imperfections are removed. Finish sanding will be done once the cabinet has been assembled.

It is necessary to drill five 3/16-inch holes through the base so that it can be screwed to the clock body. To find the locations of these holes, refer to Fig. 5-32. When the holes are drilled, use a countersink bit or a larger drill to make the recess

for the screw head. Using the quality wood glue and five 1¼-inch number-six wood screws, glue and screw the base to the clock body. Make sure the back of the base is flush with the back of the clock body (Fig. 5-33).

To mount the final to the top, you must first drill two 3/16-inch holes through the top. These holes are located by measuring in 2½ inches from the two ends and 1½ inches in from the back edge. Drill and countersink the three 3/16-inch holes. Then glue and screw the final to the top; use two 1 ¼-inch number-six wood screws.

Drill two 3/16-inch holes through the top interior horizontal support on the clock body (part B). These will be the pilot holes for the screws that hold the top and final to the clock body. A countersink is not necessary because the screw heads will be inside the clock body, out of sight. Drill these holes 1½ inches in from the front edge and 1 inch from the ends (Fig. 5-34).

Fig. 5-30. Assembling parts A and B of the bracket clock.

Fig. 5-31. Rounding the top (part C), the base (part E), and the final (part D).

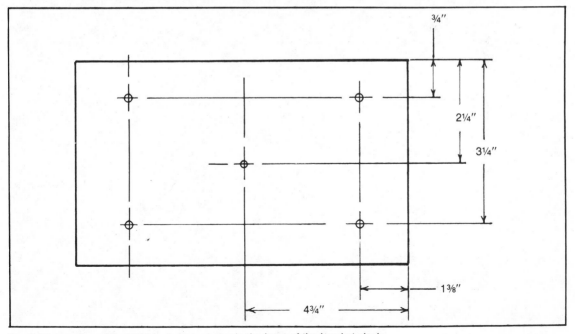

Fig. 5-32. Location of the 3/16-inch screw holes in the base of the bracket clock.

Fig. 5-33. The sides (parts A) are glued and screwed with their back edge flush with the back edges of parts C and E.

Glue and screw the top and final assembly into the clock body. Cut two ¼-×-6-×-6-inch pieces of plywood. These are the back of the clock and the dial mounting board (parts F). Drill and countersink for 3/16-inch holes ⅜ of an inch up from the bottom, ⅜ of an inch down from the top, and 1 inch in from the sides (Figs. 5-35 and 5-36). Repeat this on the other ¼-inch piece of plywood. Screw one plywood panel onto the back of the clock body using four ¾-inch number-four wood screws. This will be the only access to the clock movement. Do *not* glue it on!

Do not install the dial mounting board until the center hand-shaft hole has been drilled. The size of the hole is determined by the movement you are using. Once it is drilled, it can be glued and screwed onto the clock body using four ½-inch number-four wood screws.

Glue the dial to the front mounting board. If you are using a paper dial, do *not* use a water base glue such as Elmer's. The paper will absorb the water and stain the dial. Use rubber cement for paper dials; it can be found in the school supply

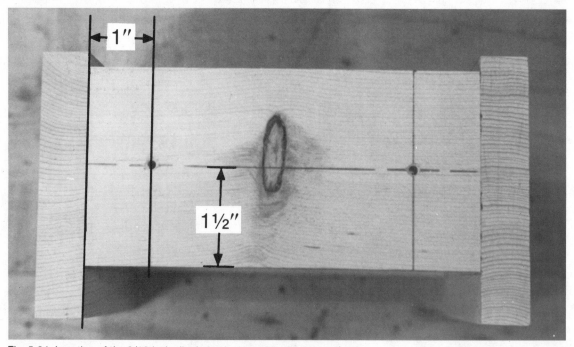

Fig. 5-34. Location of the 3/16-inch pilot holes in the top horizontal support.

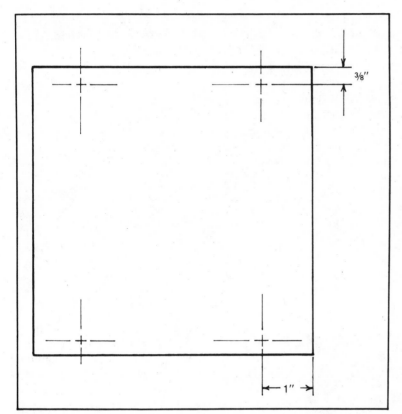

Fig. 5-35. Location of the screw holes in parts F, the clock case back, and dial mounting board.

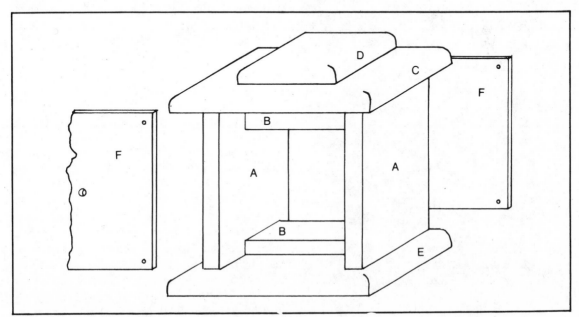

Fig. 5-36. An exploded view of the bracket clock showing its wooden parts.

section of most stores. Metal dials can also be mounted by using rubber cement, small nails, or the hand-shaft washer and nut might be all that is necessary to hold the dial to the mounting board.

The construction of the bracket clock cabinet is now complete. All that remains is the installation of the clock movement and hands. For the sample clock, two accessories were added to the finished clock. They are the small handle screwed onto the top and the antique brass feet on the base. These are optional touches that will enhance the appearance of your clock. Once you have finished this, you will have built one of America's favorite clocks. I am sure you will be happy with the results and with the many compliments you will receive from admirers. This is a clock cabinet similar to the very expensive ones sold in many stores. The craftsman should be able to build them for a fraction of the cost, making it a very profitable resale item.

Fig. 5-38. The ½" wide ¼" deep rabbet cut on the ends of parts A.

MARINE CHRONOMETER

Early sailing vessels plying the trade routes of Europe needed a method for keeping accurate time. Accurate time aboard ship was necessary to plot the stars for navigational purposes. As clock movements became more accurate, so did navigation. Improved navigation resulted in the widening of trade routes that enabled commerce to prosper. Thus, the good, sturdy marine chronometer timepiece was developed for aboard-ship use. The cabinet for this clock (Fig. 5-37) is a replica of those used in the 1790s. The movement is not a replica; it is a modern quartz battery movement.

The cabinet consists of a square box. The corners of the box can be mitered, dovetailed, or rabbeted as in this example. The front and rear (parts A) are ½ of an inch thick, 3¾ inches wide, and 6 inches long. Parts B are also ½ of an inch thick and 3¾ inches wide, but only 5½ inches long. See Table 5-6.

On the front and rear (parts A), cut a ½-inch-wide-by-¼-inch-deep rabbet on each end (Fig. 5-38). This joint is best cut with a dado blade on the table or radial-arm saw, but it can be done with a backsaw or hammer and chisel. Trial fit parts A and B together. If they fit together properly, glue them together as in Fig. 5-39. Make sure the corners are kept square while the cabinet is clamped. If it

Fig. 5-37. Marine chronometer.

Table 5-6. Marine Chronometer Materials.

Part	Quantity	Size	Description
A	2	½″ × 3¾″ × 6″	front & back
B	2	½″ × 3¾″ × 5½″	sides
C	2	⅜″ × 6″ × 6″	top & bottom
D	2	⅜″ × 2″ ×5″	dial supports
E	1	⅜″ × 5″ × 5″	dial mounting board
	1	½″ long hand-shaft	quartz movement
	1	4½″	dial and bezel
	1		set of hands to fit movement
	1		brazing rod (optional)

should be out of square, the remaining parts will not fit properly.

While the front and sides are drying, cut the top and bottom (parts C). They are ⅜ of an inch thick, 6 inches wide, and 6 inches long. These are to be glued on the clock cabinet. The grain of the top and bottom run in the same direction as the grain on the front (Fig. 5-40).

At this point the box is solid. There is no separation of top and bottom. While it is still in one piece, sand each side smooth and remove any imperfections that might have occurred at the rabbet joint. Draw a light pencil line 1⅛ inches down from the top. This line should be drawn around the box. At this line, the box will be cut into two pieces, the top and bottom. The cut can be made with a backsaw, fine-tooth handsaw, bandsaw, or on the table saw (Figs. 5-41 and 5-42).

Cut two ⅜-inch-thick-by-2-inches-wide-by-5-inches-long, dial-board supports. These will be glued inside the lower part of the box on opposite sides to support the dial board (Fig. 5-43).

The dial board (part E) is 5¼ inches by 5¼ inches by ⅜ of an inch thick. On this board, drill a ⅜-inch hole through the center. This is where the hand-shaft of the clock movement will protrude (Fig. 5-44). With the movement attached to the dial board, insert it into the box—resting it on the dial-board supports. The board should fit snug, but not so tight that it cannot be removed. The board will need to be removed from time to time to service the clock movement.

The hinges for the box should be put on, temporarily, and the hasp that holds the box should be closed. When these have been properly fitted, remove the hardware so that it will not interfere with the staining and varnishing of the box.

When the box has had ample time to dry, reinstall the hinges, hasp, and movement. Also install the dial, bezel, and clock movement hands. See Figs. 5-45 and 5-46.

The inside of the box top can be covered with velvet, as some early marine chronometers were. Possibly an engraved brass plaque can be inserted that dedicates the clock to a special person or shows a seascape. The bottom of the box should also be covered with felt so the box does not scratch the desk or table on which it is placed. Another interesting possibility would be to install campaign trunk corner hardware on the eight corners.

Fig. 5-39. Gluing parts A and B together for the marine chronometer.

Fig. 5-40. The grain of the top and bottom should run in the same direction as the grain on parts A, the front and rear.

When selecting materials to be used for this clock, be careful of the sizes. The dial and bezel should be small enough to easily fit in the box and also allow the bezel to open with ease. The movement must operate horizontally rather than vertically as they normally do when hanging on a wall. Be sure to test the movement to make sure the horizontal position will not hinder the movement operation. Most quartz movements should operate well in this manner.

The marine chronometer is only a replica of those in the past. This clock is not expected to go to sea; it will sit in a respected place on a table, desk, or mantel. The dial cannot be viewed without opening the top. This can be inconvenient at times. A 4¾-inch brazing rod, available at any welding supply store, can be used to hold the top open. The brass of the bezel ring, hasp, and top support all provide a pleasing contrast to the dark wood and velvet.

The marine chronometer is not an expensive

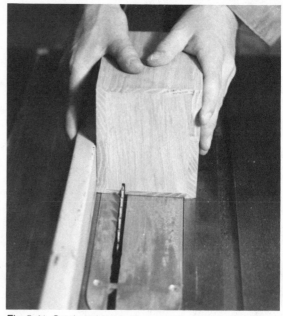

Fig. 5-41. Set the table saw fence 1⅛ inches from the blade. Make one pass cutting one side.

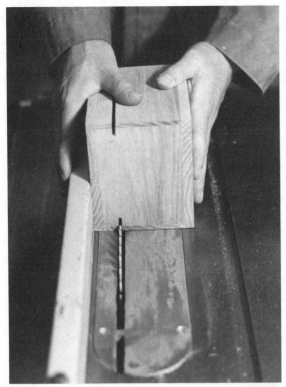

Fig. 5-42. Turn the box over and make another pass on the opposite side. Repeat this process on the other two sides to separate the top from the bottom.

Fig. 5-43. Glue the dial supports inside the lower portion of the box.

Fig. 5-44. Test fit the clock movement on the dial mounting board (photo by Oltz Studio).

clock to build. It requires a small amount of wood, a small dial, and a bezel. The bezel is an option that is not necessary, but it is a nice touch. The clock is run by a quartz battery movement that provides an accurate movement at an inexpensive price. Despite the low price tag of this clock, the result is a timepiece that would command a goodly sum if purchased in a store. This fine clock will also command a respected place in any home.

EASEL CLOCK

The easel clock (Fig. 5-47) is a replica of a type of desk clock originally built in the 1930s. Its clock

Fig. 5-45. The marine chronometer with the hardware installed, prior to the application of the velvet in the box top and mounting board (photo by Oltz Studio).

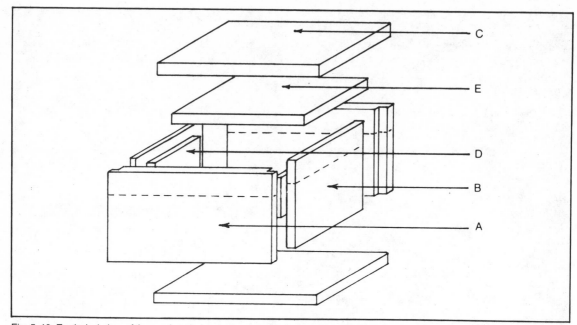

Fig. 5-46. Exploded view of the marine chronometer showing its wooden parts (dial and movement—not shown—courtesy of Klockit).

cabinet retains the smooth, graceful lines characteristic of that era, yet it has a modern and accurate quartz battery fit-up. A battery fit-up is a movement, dial, hands, and glass bezel all in one compact unit.

The fit-up used for this project has a 2½-inch-diameter dial. If the fit-up selected for use is larger or smaller, alterations will have to be made in the clock case.

There are three parts (A, B, and C) to the clock case body, all of them identical. These pieces measure ¾ of an inch thick, 3¾ inches wide, and 4

inches long. See Table 5-7. The center of the movement hole is located 1⅞ inches in from the sides and 1 13/16 inches up from the bottom (Fig. 5-48). Cut out the hole for the movement. In this

Table 5-7. Easel Clock Materials.

Part	Quantity	Size	Description
A	1	¾″ × 3¾″ × 4″	clock body front
B	1	¾″ × 3¾″ × 4″	clock body
C	1	¾″ × 3¾″ × 4″	clock body
D	1	½″ × 3⅜″ × 6¼″	base
E	2	½″ × 1″ × 2¼″	risers
	2	1¼″, number eight	roundhead screws
	2	1″, number six	flathead screws
	2	½″	buttons (optional)
	1	2¾″ diameter	clock fit-up

Fig. 5-47. Easel clock.

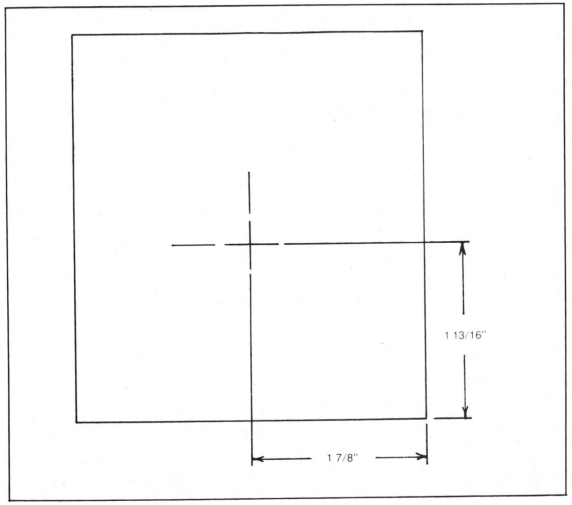

Fig. 5-48. Locating the hand-shaft hole on the easel clock cabinet.

case, the movement requires a 2½-inch-diameter hole. Cut the hole through all three pieces. Test the clock fit-up in the hole and make any necessary corrections at this time.

Draw the outline of the peaked top on the three clock body parts (A, B, and C). This can be drawn by using the ½-inch square grid pattern shown in Fig. 5-49. Lay this out on a piece of cardboard. Then trace it onto parts A, B, and C. Using a coping saw, or any other saw capable of cutting curves, cut the peak design out of each of parts A, B, and C. Do not sand the cut parts at this point.

Glue the three parts together—selecting the piece with the most pleasing grain pattern—for the front of the clock body (Fig. 5-50). After the clock body assembly has completely dried, file and sand all three parts at once. This will ensure that the pieces will match.

The remaining three pieces are all ½-inch thick. The base (part D) is 3⅜ inches wide by 6¼ inches long. The ends of the base should be square to the edges, but there is a decorative cutout along the front edge. The cutout is shown on the ½-inch grid pattern in Fig. 5-51. All of the edges, except the back, are gently rounded. This can be done with a file or coarse sandpaper.

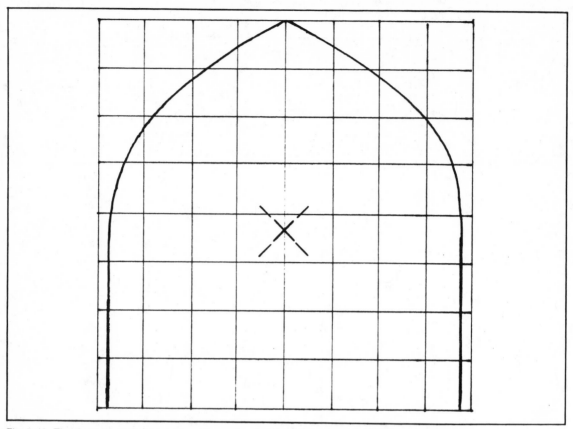

Fig. 5-49. The three-peaked clock body parts can be drawn out by using this ½-inch grid pattern.

Fig. 5-50. The glued-up clock body of the easel clock.

The two risers (parts E) measure ½-inch thick, 1¼ inches wide, and 2¼ inches long. These two parts are curved as shown in the ½-inch grid pattern in Fig. 5-52. While drawing out the curve, also mark the location for the center hole. Cut and shape these two parts. At the center hole location, drill a 3/16-inch-diameter hole through both risers.

On the base, measure in ¾ of an inch from both ends and draw a light line. Measure in from the edges along these lines 1 11/16 inches. This should mark the center of the board (Fig. 5-53). At these two points, drill a ⅛-inch diameter hole through the base. On the bottom of the base, countersink the holes so the head of a number-six screw will fit flush with the bottom of the base (Fig. 5-54).

On the bottom of the risers locate the center. At this point, drill a small, 3/32-inch-diameter hole about ¾ of an inch deep (Fig. 5-55). Using the

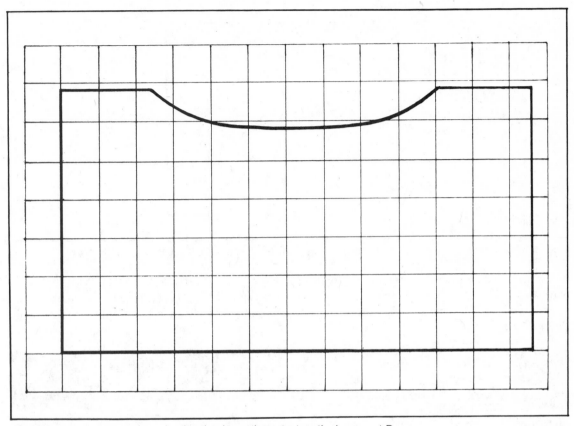

Fig. 5-51. A ½-inch grid pattern showing the decorative cutout on the base, part D.

1-inch-long, number-six flathead screws, attach the risers to the base. First fit them together with screws only. If they fit together properly, then glue and screw the risers to the base.

On the clock front, measure up from the bottom 1¼ inches and 1⅛ inches in from the front surface (Fig. 5-56). At this point, drill a 3/32-inch hole through the cabinet to the clock fit-up hole. Do this on both sides of the clock body.

All that remains is to apply a suitable finish and assemble the clock body between the risers. In the original, the clock body was held between the risers with roundhead screws; the head is left exposed for decorative purposes. If this is not preferred, the head of the screw can be recessed below the surface of the riser and covered with a dowel or furniture button.

The easel clock is a small desk clock that is a

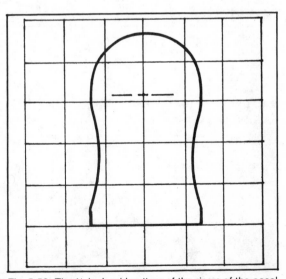

Fig. 5-52. The ½-inch grid pattern of the risers of the easel clock showing its shape.

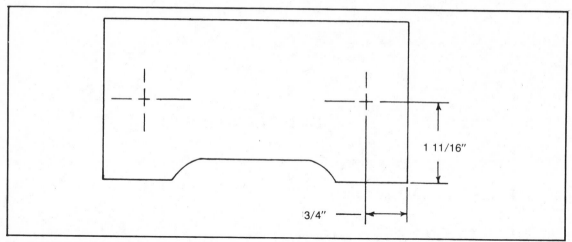

Fig. 5-53. Drill two ⅛-inch holes through the base for the risers to be screwed to the base at these locations.

nonintrusive obstruction. Because it is easy to build and uses a quartz clock fit-up, this clock is very well suited to be mass produced for the resale market. See Fig. 5-57.

NAUTICAL DESK CLOCK

The nautical desk clock (Fig. 5-58) is a simple clock built of only three pieces of wood; yet it is highly attractive. Because this clock relies on a very small

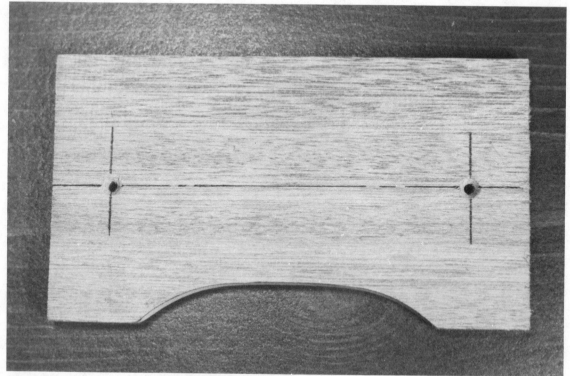

Fig. 5-54. The holes through the base will need to be countersunk on the bottom edge so that the screw heads are set below the surface.

Fig. 5-55. Drill a 3/32-inch-diameter pilot hole in the base of the risers.

amount of wood, an expensive species of wood can be used. The result will be an attractive and still overall inexpensive desk clock. The sample was built using one piece of ¾-inch-thick-4-inches-wide-by-20-inches-long piece of kiln-dried black walnut.

Construction begins by cutting all three pieces. The base (part A) is ¾ of an inch thick, 4 inches wide, and 10 inches long. The two risers (parts B) are ¾ of an inch thick, 4 inches wide, and 5 inches long. See Table 5-8.

Glue the two parts B together. These are glued surface to surface (Fig. 5-59). While the riser assembly is drying, sand the surfaces, ends, and edges of the base. Because this clock has been designed with squared edges—unlike many of the clocks in this book with routed edges—care must be taken to keep the edges from being rounded while sanding.

On the ends of the riser assembly, draw a

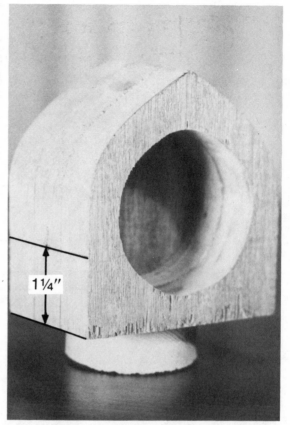

Fig. 5-56. Drill a 3/32-inch hole 1 1/8 inches in from the front edge and 1 1/4 inches up from the bottom of the clock body.

diagonal line from one corner to the other (Fig. 5-60). Cut the riser assembly along the diagonal line. This can be done most efficiently with a bandsaw, but almost any saw can be used. Sand the slanted surface of the riser to a smooth, flat surface free of saw and sanding marks.

The major woodworking operation of this attractive desk clock has been completed. All that remains is to glue the riser assembly to the base. The riser is glued and clamped on the left end of the base and left to dry. When the parts are glued and dried, apply the finish of your choice.

The movement used on the nautical desk clock is a small, 2¾-inch-diameter, quartz-clock, bezel fit-up. These types of movements are usually inserted into a hole drilled in a piece of wood like the one in the easel clock. On this clock, an optional

Table 5-8. Nautical Desk Clock Materials.

Part	Quantity	Size	Description
A	1	¾″ × 4″ × 10″	base
B	2	¾″ × 4″ × 5″	riser
	1	2½″ dial	quartz bezel fit-up
	1		nautical base for movement
	1		small deck cleat or any brass nautical fixture

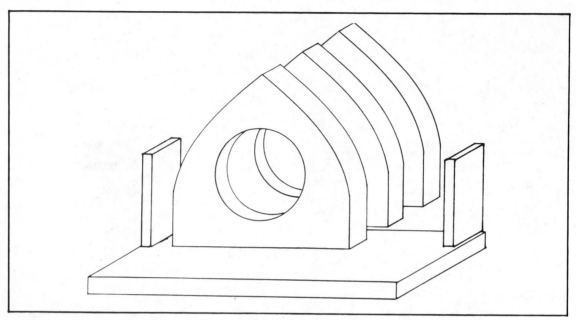

Fig. 5-57. An exploded view of the easel clock showing its wood component parts.

Fig. 5-58. Nautical desk clock.

Fig. 5-59. Glue the two ¾-×-4-×-5-inch riser parts surface to surface.

Fig. 5-61. Center the nautical-style clock case in the wood riser, and then attach it to the riser with nails or screws.

clock case is used to house the movement fit-up. It is the clock case that presents the nautical appearance to the clock. The clock case is centered in the wood riser and then screwed or nailed in place (Fig. 5-61).

Small brass *brads* can be used to nail the case in place of softwoods. With hardwoods, small brass *screws* should be used. A view of the wooden parts used are shown in Fig. 5-62.

The 5-inch-long flat surface of the base can be left empty or you can have a decorative brass figure attached to it. The desk clock shown in Fig. 5-63 has a small brass deck cleat centered in the area.

Other ideas that will be attractive are shown in Figs. 5-64 and 5-65. Still another pleasing effect would be the addition of a pen and pencil set. The pen and pencil sets may be purchased from several of the suppliers found in the clock suppliers chapter.

The nautical clock is an attractive clock that will be a welcome addition to the desk of any nautical-minded person. Attaching almost any figure, statue, corporate logo, or engraved brass plate makes it a clock the craftsman will enjoy giving.

Fig. 5-60. After the ends of the riser have been sanded even, draw a diagonal line from corner to corner.

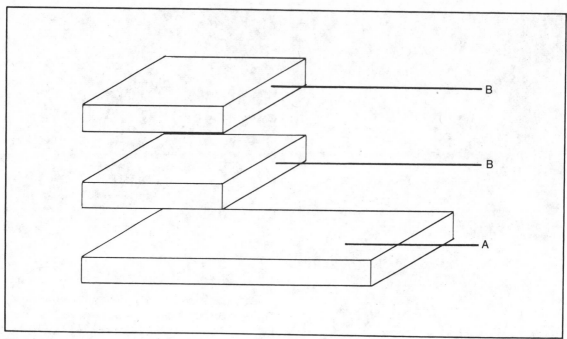

Fig. 5-62. An exploded view of the nautical desk clock, showing its wood parts. (The quartz clock bezel fit-up and optional case are courtesy of Klockit.)

Fig. 5-63. A small brass deck cleat and pen can be mounted on the desk clock for decoration.

Fig. 5-64. A brass sailboat can be glued to the desk clock.

Fig. 5-65. Almost anything can be mounted on the desk clock. Here a small statue is glued in place.

Chapter 6

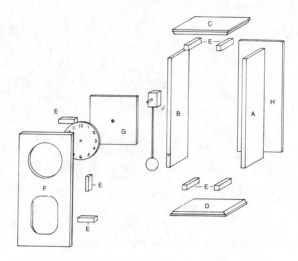

Wall Clocks

THE VAST MAJORITY OF CLOCKS FOUND IN homes today are hung on the walls. Wall clocks have evolved for two reasons. Historically, clocks were hung to provide space below for the weight shells to drop. More recently, though, the clock has become an integral part of a home's decor. As a result, today's wall clocks combine the functionality of quality clock works with a handsome clock cabinet that lends its design to the decor of the room rather than detracting from it.

This chapter contains a wide variety of wall clock styles. There are relatively simple designs requiring little or no experience, clocks with a modern appearance for the home decor, and clocks that are replicas of the classic ones of the past. Many of these clocks can be built with hand tools generally found in the home, but there are others that require the use of woodworking machines.

EASY PENDULUM WALL CLOCK

As its name indicates, the clock shown in Fig. 6-1 is easy to make. Its design and warm, rich appearance

are attractive. The easy pendulum wall clock is similar to the three-piece wall clock found in this chapter; they share the same basic method of construction. They are also similar in that an almost limitless amount of designs can be created on the front-face and back-panel sections.

The example that follows incorporates the characteristics of two furniture styles. It uses the sharp edges and straight lines commonly found in modern furniture, and the curved edges, rounded corners, and pendulum movement that are often found in early American clocks. These characteristics are combined to produce an attractive clock.

Select two pieces of wood with a measurement of ¾ of an inch thick, 8 inches wide, and 11 inches long. One of these will become the back panel (part B), and the other will become the front face, (part A). See Tables 6-1 and 6-2. Both of these pieces will be cut to similar designs; it will be easiest to temporarily tack these together with 1¼ inch nails. Nail them together from the back panel so that, when the nails are removed, the nail holes will not

Fig. 6-1. Easy pendulum wall clock.

Table 6-1. Easy Pendulum Wall Clock Materials.

Part	Quantity	Size	Description
A	1	¾" × 8¾" × 14⅞"	front
B	2	¾" × 2" × 12½"	sides
C	1	¾" × 6½" × 12½"	back
	4	1½" number six	flathead screws
	1	hand-shaft to fit ¾" dial thickness	battery movement
	1	8 inch	pendulum
	1	6½" diameter	dial or bezel
	1		set of hands to fit dial

meet, set the point of your compass and draw a ¾-inch radius arc (Fig. 6-4). The same ¾-inch radius is used to draw the rounding of the bottom peak, where the two 45-degree lines meet. Before you cut this lower ¾-inch arc, reset your compass, and draw a 4-inch radius arc. Cutting close to the lines, but not on them, cut the ¾-inch rounds at the corners. Do not cut the 4-inch radius line.

The similarity between the front face and back panel ends at this point. It is time to separate them and treat each as an individual piece. The back panel (part B) is complete other than drilling four, 3/16-inch holes in it. These holes will later be used to screw the back and sides together. These will be drilled 1⅜ inches in from the sides. Two of the holes are 1 inch down from the top; the other two are 6 inches down from the top (Fig. 6-5).

Set the back panel aside and begin work on the front piece. Measure over from the side 4 inches and down from the top 3 inches. Where the two lines cross is the location the hand shaft hole will be drilled. Drill the ⅜-inch, hand-shaft hole (Fig. 6-6). Most movements have hand shafts that will fit

Table 6-2. Easy Pendulum Wall Clock Alternate Design Materials.

Part	Quantity	Size	Description
A	1	¾" × 8¾" × 14⅞"	front
B	2	¾" × 2" × 12½"	sides
C	1	¾" × 6½" × 12½"	back
	4	1½", number six	flathead screws
	1	long shaft	battery movement
	1	8 inch	pendulum
	1	6½" diameter	dial or bezel
	1		set of hands to fit dial

show on the front face. To prevent nail holes from being visible on the lower portion of the back panel, do not nail lower than 5½ inches below the top edge (Fig. 6-2).

It is rather easy to lay out the design for these two boards because you will be doing both of them at the same time. Measure up from the bottom 4 inches and draw a light pencil line across the board. From the point where this line touches the two outside edges, draw a 45-degree line down toward the bottom edge (Fig. 6-3). These two 45 degree lines should meet in the middle of the bottom edge. Remove the excess wood by cutting close to the 45-degree lines, but not on them. This will allow you material to file and sand (Fig. 6-3).

The rounding of the two upper corners is accomplished by first measuring down and over from the corner ¾ of an inch. Where these two lines

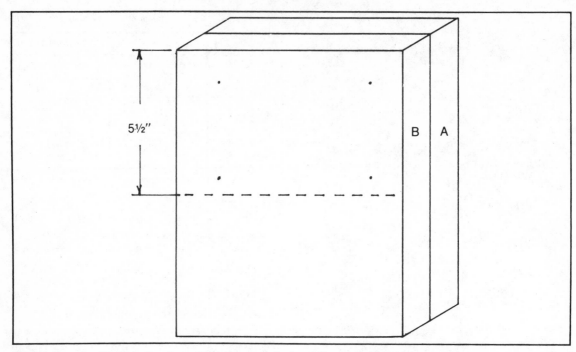

Fig. 6-2. Do not nail below a line drawn 5½ inches from the top end on parts A and B.

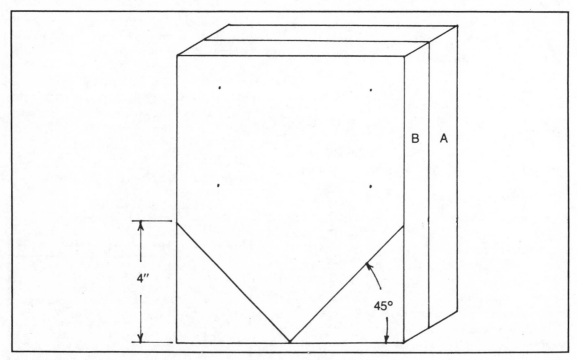

Fig. 6-3. The lay-out lines drawn on parts A and B of the easy pendulum wall clock.

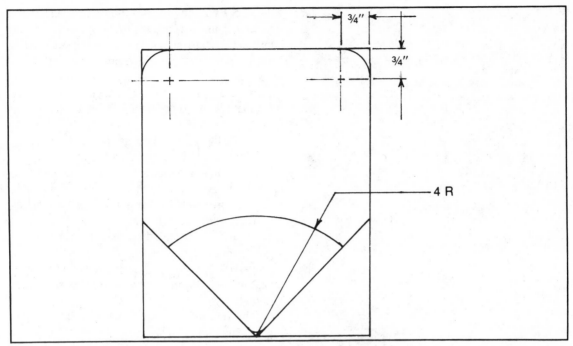

Fig. 6-4. This drawing indicates the location to draw the various radii on the clock front.

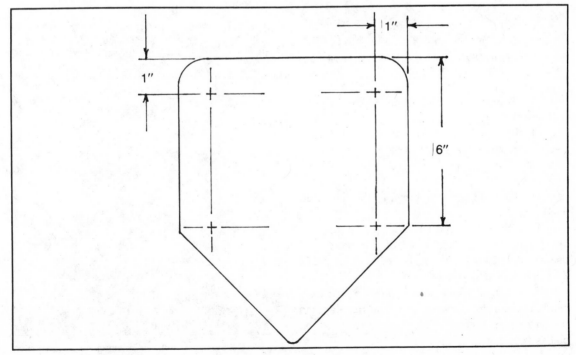

Fig. 6-5. Lay out the location of the 3/16-inch drill holes on the back, part B.

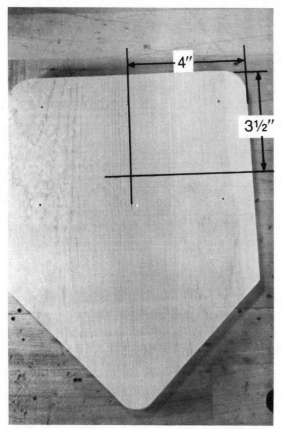

Fig. 6-6. Location of the hand-shaft hole to be drilled through part A of the easy pendulum wall clock.

through a ⅜-inch hole, but check the movement that will be used for the exact size.

The front piece, up to this point, has been the same shape and size as the back panel. The two will now differ because the 4-inch-radius arc drawn on the bottom of the front is cut out. Cut close to the line, and then file and sand down to the line (Fig. 6-7).

The two sides (parts C) required for this project are ¾-inch-thick wood of the same type used for the rest of the clock. These sides should be 2 inches wide and 7 inches long.

Now that all of the wood pieces of the easy pendulum wall clock have been cut and shaped, sand the surfaces of each piece. It is easier to sand the pieces before it is assembled.

Just as with the three-piece wall clock, the two

side pieces will be glued to the front face. Draw a light pencil line on the *rear* surface of the front piece 1 inch in from both side edges. Glue the sides to the front-face piece at these two lines. Allow them to dry (Fig. 6-8).

It is advisable to trial assemble the clock movement at this time. If for some reason the parts don't fit together properly, it is best to correct it now before the stain and varnish are applied. Figure 6-9 shows an exploded view of the clock.

After installing the clock movement, screw the back in place using four 1¼-inch, number-six flathead screws. Countersink the screw heads below the surface of the part C.

Once you are satisfied that the parts fit together properly, remove the clock back and stain each part. It is easier and neater to stain the clock disassembled. Varnishing can be done after final assembly.

The type of dial you use can be almost any style. This example has a 6-inch round dial, but hour markers can also be used to create appealing and interesting designs. Look in the Dial and Face chapter for useful ideas.

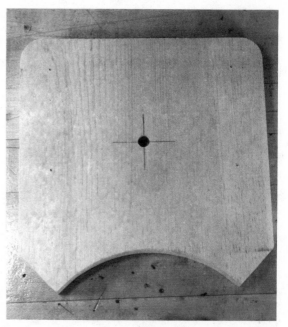

Fig. 6-7. Cut the clock front, part A, along the curved line on the lower portion.

Fig. 6-8. The sides, parts C, must be glued on the rear of part A, the clock front, 1 inch in from both edges.

As you can see, this beautiful clock can be created with very little wood and a little time. Because of its low cost and ease of construction, this clock is a good project to produce in numbers for holiday gift giving or for resale (Fig. 6-10).

LOG ROUND CLOCK

A log round is a cross section of a tree trunk or limb. The log can be almost any size, but a minimum of 6 inches in diameter is recommended. The 6-inch minimum has been selected because this is the smallest round that lends itself to clock construction.

A log round can be cut from any type of hardwood or softwood tree. Experimentation can help you find the type of grain pattern that is most appealing. Walnut, maple, or oak look nice, and many of the pines also make good choices because of their coloration and contrast between the annual rings and the lighter-colored spring wood.

Almost any type of saw can be used to cut the rounds. Powered saws such as chain saws and band

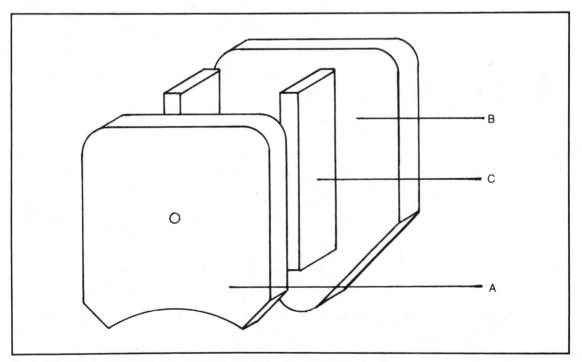

Fig. 6-9. Exploded view of the easy pendulum wall clock, showing the wood parts.

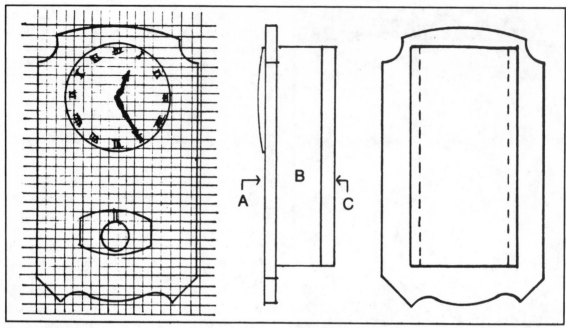

Fig. 6-10. This clock is made using the same methods as the easy pendulum wall clock.

saws will do the job fast and easy. If you do not have these, a sharp handsaw can be used. The sawing will be a long process if the log you are using is freshly cut. The moisture will cause the saw blade

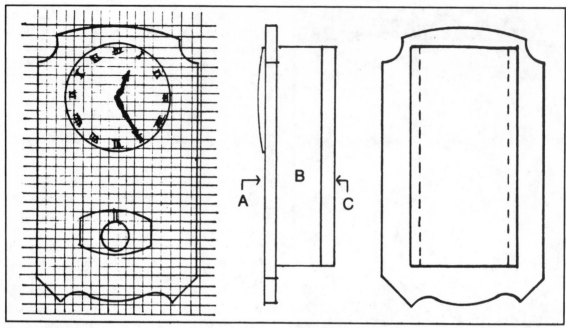

Fig. 6-11. Log round clock.

to stick. When the log round dries out, there is a good chance that it will crack or split. To help prevent the log from cracking, select a log that has dried for several months before cutting. Then cut the round from the middle of the log. The ends usually have cracks or splits in them. The log round should be approximately 2 inches thick. Anything thinner will not allow enough room for the clock movement.

The only real work in building this clock (Fig. 6-11), after the round has been cut, is cutting the recess in the back for the clock movement and sanding the front surface. The easiest way to cut out the recess in the back of the movement is by using a router. If no router is available, the next best way is to use a large drill bit to make several holes in the area that is to be removed (Fig. 6-12). Then use a chisel and mallet to remove any remaining wood. The thickness at the recess should be no more than ¾ of an inch.

Locate the center of the log round by approximating it with a ruler. Do not expect the center of the annual rings to be the center of the log round. Trees do not always grow completely round.

Fig. 6-12. Drilling several holes in the movement recess is one way to remove a large amount of wood quickly.

Table 6-3. Log Round Clock Materials.

Quantity	Size	Description
1	6″ minimum diameter by 2″ thick	log round
1		battery movement
1		set of hands to fit
1		set of hour markers, your choice

Drill out the center hole large enough for the hand-shaft of the movement to fit through. The size to drill will have to be determined by your particular movement. The size is usually ⅜ of an inch.

Sand the front surface using various grades of sandpaper. If there are large ridges left from the saw, it will be necessary to use a file or plane to remove them before sanding. Sand until all imperfections and scratches are gone and the surface is smooth.

The finish you use is determined by your choice. Varnish will be all that is necessary if there

Fig. 6-13. The log round clock and the alternate log slab clock.

is a pleasing grain pattern. If the log round seems to lack color or contrast in color, you might want to stain the surface.

The only step left is to install the movement and apply the hour markers. Using one of the methods described in the chapter on faces and dials, locate the hour positions and mark them with nails, commercially produced markers, or anything else you prefer.

A simple variation of the log round clock is the log slab clock. Rather than cutting the log into a cross section, the log is cut lengthwise. This is best done with a chain saw. Cut out the clock movement cavity and drill the hand-shaft hole (as described for the log round). The bark should be covered with a varnish finish to avoid chipping and peeling. Although an easy variation, this makes a clock that gives a very different appearance than the log round clock. Both are shown in Fig. 6-13.

Fig. 6-14. Three-piece wall clock.

Table 6-4. Three-Piece Wall Clock.

Part	Quantity	Size	Description
A	1	¾″ × 8″ × 10″	face
B	2	¾″ × 2″ × 6″	sides
	1	hand-shaft suitable for a ¾″ dial thickness	battery movement (8″ to 10″ pendulum is optional)
	1		set of hands to fit movement and dial
	1		dial, 6″ diameter, or other method of marking hours

THREE-PIECE WALL CLOCK

This section deals with a rather simple method of building an attractive wall clock. Any type of movement can be used—electric, wind-up, or battery. The following specific instructions have been designed to use battery movements (other movements may require slight variations in size or construction).

One thing nice about the clock shown in Fig. 6-14 is its flexibility. The front can be cut into virtually any shape. You need not be bound to the shape and size of the clocks described here. Limitless amounts of designs of the three-piece wall clock can be made. Variations are found in clock stores at outrageous prices, but it is actually an inexpensive and relatively simple clock to build.

To begin building the clock pictured, select a piece of wood that is ¾ of an inch thick, 8 inches wide, and 10 inches long (part A). This will become the face of the clock. Make sure it has a pleasing grain and no defects that will ruin its finished appearance.

Draw a very light line from the upper left corner to the lower right corner. Do this again from the upper right to the lower left. Where these two lines cross is the center of the board (Fig. 6-15).

Set a compass for a radius of 5 inches. Placing the point in the center (where the pencil lines cross), draw an arc from the middle of each board out to the top and bottom of the board. At this time, drill out the ⅜-inch, hand-shaft hole. This will be drilled in the center of the board. Cut slightly outside the two arcs and file down to the pencil lines.

The outside edge can be sanded and left with the sharp edge, rounded edge, or a fancy routed edge. Do this to suit your taste.

Cut two ¾- × -2- × -6-inch pieces of wood (parts

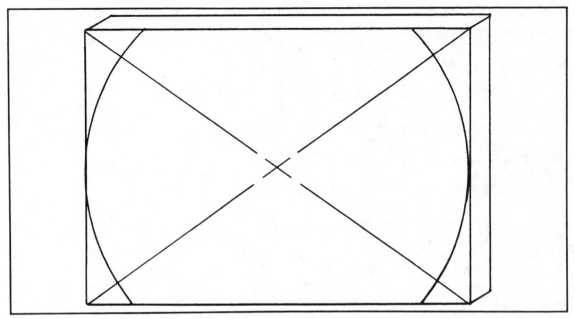

Fig. 6-15. The crossed diagonal lines form the center for the 5-inch-radius arcs.

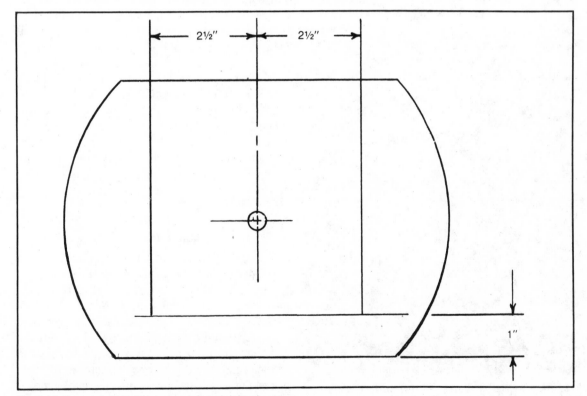

Fig. 6-16. Draw two lines 2½ inches left and right of center.

B). These should be made from the same type of wood as used for the clock face. See Table 6-4. Because the ends and outsides of these pieces can be seen from the sides, be sure to sand them carefully.

On the back of the clock face, draw a pencil line through the center from edge to edge. From that line, measure over 2½ inches in both directions and draw two lines parallel to the center line (Fig. 6-16). The two outside lines show where the two ¾-×-2-×-6-inch pieces are to be glued. Apply glue to edges of both side pieces, and align them along the two outside lines as shown in Fig. 6-17. The ends of the side pieces should be set back from the edge of the face by 1 inch.

This can be clamped very simply by laying a board across both side pieces and placing a heavy object on top of it. Allow this to dry completely before going any further. The face should be sanded to remove any scratches and imperfections. When sanding, be careful not to round the edges (if the edges are to remain squared).

When the final sanding is completed, the woodworking portion of this clock is done. All that remains is to apply some type of finish. It can be anything from varnish to paint. It really doesn't

Fig. 6-17. Locate the two sides along the lines previously drawn.

Table 6-5. Three-Piece Wall Clock Alternate Design Materials.

Quantity	Size	Description
1	¾" × 10" × 10"	face
2	¾" × 2" × 6"	sides
1	8" to 10" pendulum (optional)	battery movement with long hand-shaft
1		set of hands sized to fit
1	6" to 8" diameter	dial (or other method to mark hours)

matter, but apply it before the dial or hour markers are attached. See Fig. 6-18.

Almost any type of dial can be used. The clock in the instructions has been designed to use a 6-inch-diameter round dial, although a dial with a glass bezel might be just the added touch you are looking for. These dials involve some expense, but there are less expensive ways to mark the hours. These methods are described in detail in Chapter 3.

The clock shown in this section has a pendulum wagging below the clock face. The pendulum is an option. This clock can also be built without a pendulum movement or it could have false or functional weight shells hanging below.

The three-piece wall clock allows the wood craftsman a great deal of flexibility. See Fig. 6-19. The wood front face can be cut in almost any shape. An interesting idea would be to make the face from wood floor tiles. Beautiful wood parquet tiles can be purchased from stores that sell floor coverings. The movement can be of almost any type, and for the dial or hour markers the possibilities are limitless. With these qualities, this clock is sure to become one of your favorite projects.

WAG-ON-WALL CLOCK

The wag-on-wall clock (Fig. 6-20) is a replica of a very popular clock of America's past; it dates back to the early 1820s. Its popularity was a result of a blend of its neat, simplistic good looks and its affordable price. The clock originally was run by a spring-operated movement that required periodic winding. This replica has been designed to use one of today's accurate battery-pendulum movements or one of the newer improved spring-driven movements.

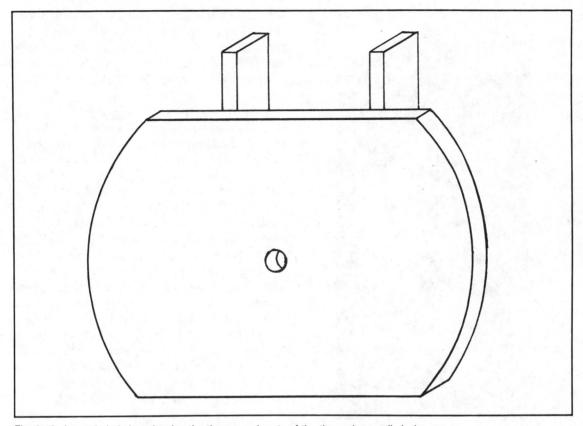

Fig. 6-18. An exploded view showing the three wood parts of the three-piece wall clock.

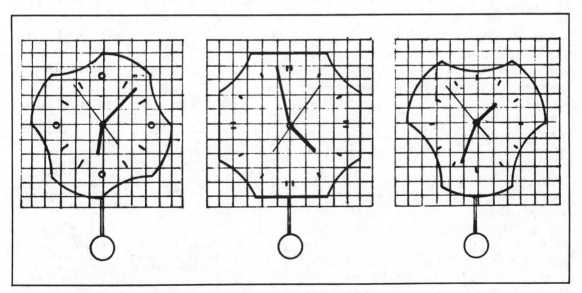

Fig. 6-19. Three examples of alternate designs to the three-piece wall clock.

Fig. 6-20. Wag-on-wall clock.

The clock cabinet has been designed to be built with materials that can be found at local lumberyards. See Table 6-6. All of the wood parts, except the door, are made of ¾-inch-thick wood. The door parts are ½ of an inch thick. If the craftsman does not have facilities to plane ¾-inch-thick wood to the ½-inch thickness, most lumberyards usually have a surface planer and they will do the job for a slight price.

Begin construction by selecting a piece of wood for the back panel (part A). This should be ¾ of an inch thick, 8¾ inches wide, and 18½ inches long. The bottom edge of the back is left straight; the top edge will be cut to the shape shown in the grid pattern (Fig. 6-21). Draw the design onto a piece of cardboard, cut it out, and then transfer the design to the board. Using either a power or hand-

saw, cut out the shape. File and sand the cut design until it is free from saw marks and smooth. The hanging hole at the top of the back board is ½ of an inch in diameter, drilled through. The location of this hole can be determined from the grid pattern (Fig 6-21).

Cut the two parts B. They are ¾ of an inch thick, 2 inches wide, and 10⅛ inches long. Also cut to size the cabinet top and bottom (parts C and D). These two parts are the same size, ¾ of an inch thick, 2 inches wide, and 7¼ inches long. Part D, the cabinet bottom, differs from the top by having a pendulum shaft hole cut (Fig. 6-22). The size of the pendulum cutout should be large enough for most movements. In the event that it is too small, the cutout can be enlarged with no ill effects.

The clock cabinet can be assembled in many ways. The cabinet sides (parts B) can be nailed, screwed, doweled, or glued to the top and bottom. The easiest method is to nail the cabinet together, but the nail heads might detract from the clock's good looks. Glueing has been chosen as the method of assembly although it will not be as strong as it would if it were screwed together. Because this plan calls for the addition of dial supports (parts E) in the cabinet corners, the cabinet will be increased in strength (Fig. 6-23).

Part F is the dial-mounting board. It can be made from either ¼-inch-thick plywood or Masonite. The dial will be mounted to this board. It provides a good surface for the dial and a sturdy mounting board for the clock movement. The dial-

Table 6-6. Wag-on-Wall Clock Materials.

Part	Quantity	Size	Description
A	1	3/4″ × 8 3/4″ × 18 1/2″	cabinet back
B	2	3/4″ × 2″ × 10 1/8″	cabinet sides
C	1	3/4″ × 2″ × 7 1/4″	cabinet top
D	1	3/4″ × 2″ × 7 1/4″	cabinet bottom
E	4	3/4″ × 3/4″ × 1 3/4″	dial supports
F	1	1/4″ × 7 3/16″ × 8 5/8″	dial mounting board
G	2	1/2″ × 1 3/8″ × 10 1/8″	door sides
H	1	1/2″ × 2 3/4″ × 6″	door top
I	1	1/2″ × 1 3/8″ × 6″	door bottom
	4	3/4″, number six	flathead screws
	4	1 1/2″, number six	flathead screws
	1	9 1/2″ to 11″ pendulum	clock movement
	1	6″ square by 1 7/8″	raised arch dial
	1		set of hands to fit dial

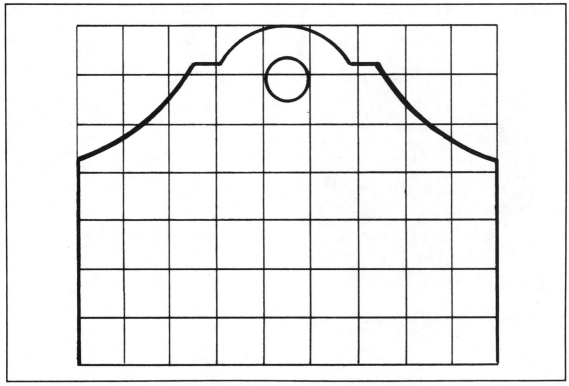

Fig. 6-21. A 1-inch grid pattern showing the design of the top of the wag-on-wall back panel.

mounting board (part F) measures 7 3/16 inches by 8⅝ inches. This fits into the cabinet, resting on the dial supports (parts E).

Drill four ⅛-inch holes through the dial-mounting board into the dial supports. These are the screw holes that will later attach the dial mounting board to the dial supports with four ¾-inch-long, number-six flathead screws. The hand shaft of the clock movement requires a ⅜-inch diameter hole to be drilled through the dial mounting board. The location of the hole can be located by measuring 3⅝ inches up from the bottom and 3 9/16 inches in from the side (Fig. 6-24).

Lay the cabinet assembly on the back board,

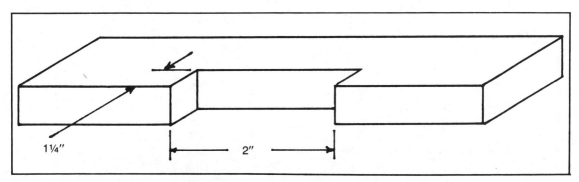

Fig. 6-22. The bottom of the cabinet has a 2-inch-by-1¼-inch pendulum hole cut. This permits the pendulum shaft to swing freely below the cabinet.

Fig. 6-23. The cabinet of the wag-on-wall clock is reinforced by gluing dial supports in the corners.

part A. The bottom of the cabinet, part D, should be 5½ inches up from the bottom edge back board. As shown in Fig. 6-25, lightly trace the outline of the cabinet onto the back board. Remove the cabinet assembly to inspect the pencil lines. At the four corners where the dial support blocks appear, drill a ⅛ inch diameter hole. It is through these four holes that the cabinet will be held to the back board with four 1½ inch, number six flathead screws (Fig. 6-26). Do not assemble the two units until both the cabinet and back board have been finish sanded. It's easier to sand the parts separately than once assembled.

This clock has a door on the front of the cabinet. The door is made up of four parts. Two parts measure ½ of an inch thick, 1⅜ inches wide, and 10⅛ inches long (parts G). Part H, the top door rail, is ½ of an inch thick, 2¾ inches wide, and 6 inches long. The bottom rail is also ½ of an inch thick and 6 inches long, but it is 1⅜ inches wide.

The top door rail has a curve cut from its lower edge. This is cut out to display the raised arch (which is part of the decorative dial). Do not draw

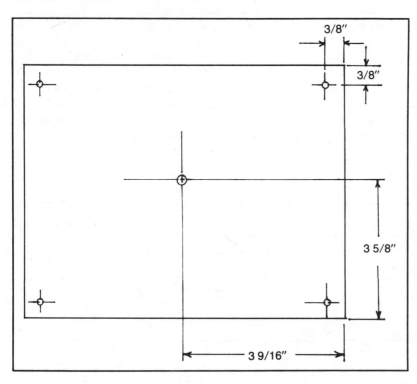

Fig. 6-24. This drawing shows the locations of the clock hand-shaft hole and the mounting-screw pilot holes.

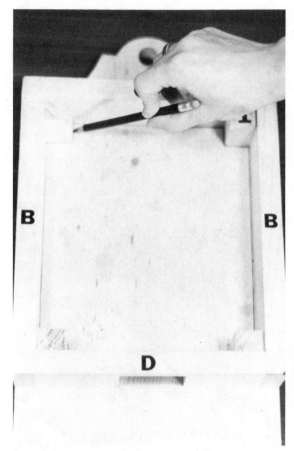

Fig. 6-25. Trace the outline of the clock cabinet onto the cabinet back.

board into the box (resting it on the dial supports as shown in Fig. 6-29). Use the four ¾-inch, number-six flathead screws to secure the mounting board to the corner blocks.

Next, screw the back (part A) onto the cabinet box. Again, similar to the dial mounting board, screw through the back into the dial supports (Fig. 6-30). See also Fig. 6-31. Make certain that the heads of the screws are countersunk below the surface of the wood just deep enough so that the heads will not be protruding and scratching the wall.

Carefully lay the door frame on the box assembly. Decide where the hinges will be placed and install them. The hinges will not be supporting much weight and will probably not be opened often. Because there is no glass in the door, the door is

this arch until you have the dial to determine its shape. The company where the dial is purchased might refer to the dial as having a 1⅞-inch raised arch, but the arch does *not* have a 1⅞-inch radius! It is best to lay the dial on the top rail and trace its outline (Fig. 6-27). After drawing the arch, cut, file, and sand the arch smooth. Lay the four door parts on a flat surface. Fit the parts together while checking for fit. If all parts fit correctly, carefully glue the door together (Fig. 6-28).

All of the major parts of the clock cabinet are made and ready for assembly. Begin the assembly by placing the clock movement hand-shaft through the hole in the mounting hole and also through the clock dial. Tighten the nut on the hand-shaft that holds the movement in place. Lay the mounting

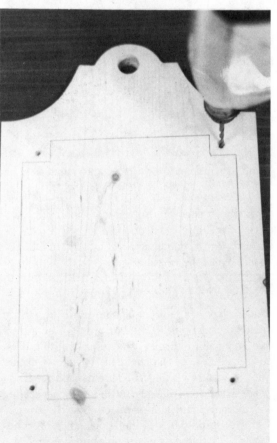

Fig. 6-26. Drill a ⅛-inch hole through the back.

Fig. 6-27. To determine the contour of the raised arch, it is easiest to trace the dial directly onto the door top.

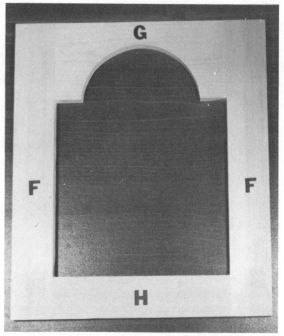

Fig. 6-28. Glue the four parts of the door together.

primarily for decorative purposes. Small butt hinges can be cut into the door and frame or decorative butterfly hinges can be used. A method to lock the door will also be needed.

SHADOW-BOX CLOCK

Shadow boxes are a popular furniture accessory found in many homes. The box provides an attractive method to display knick-knacks, thimbles, pewter figures, or just about any small collectible. The clock shown in Fig. 6-33 has carried the traditional shadow box one step further by incorporating a clock movement into one section of the box.

The shadow box in these plans has been designed with random-size openings to accommodate various-size collectibles. These are not, by any

Fig. 6-29. Assemble the dial-mounting board to the cabinet by screwing them together with four, number-six, ¾-inch screws.

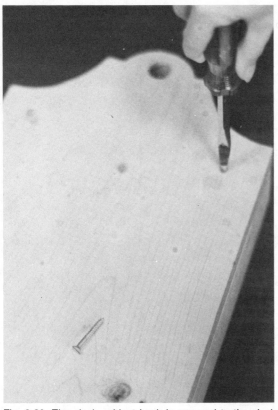

Fig. 6-30. The clock cabinet back is screwed to the clock cabinet.

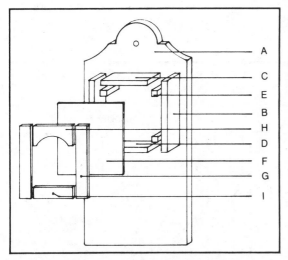

Fig. 6-31. Exploded view of the wooden parts that make up the wag-on-wall clock. (The dial and movement are courtesy of Klockit.)

A

C
E

B

H
D

F
G

I

Fig. 6-32. Shadow-box clock.

¼"

Fig. 6-33. Boards fit into the ¼-inch-deep dado providing a strong joint.

means, the only size openings. Shadow boxes may be built with any size compartments.

Construction on the shadow box color should begin by constructing the four sides of the box. This requires two parts A, that are ½ of an inch thick, 2½ inches wide, and 11 inches long, and two parts B, that measure 2½ inches wide and 17½ inches long. See Table 6-7.

The box in the sample has ¼-inch-deep-by-½-inch wide dado joints cut into parts A to hold the box together and also to hold several other horizontal pieces. These dado joints are not necessary to build the box. It could be nailed and glued or screwed and glued together. But the lengths of pieces that fit into the dado will need to be reduced by the depth of the dado, which is ¼ of an inch (Fig. 6-33).

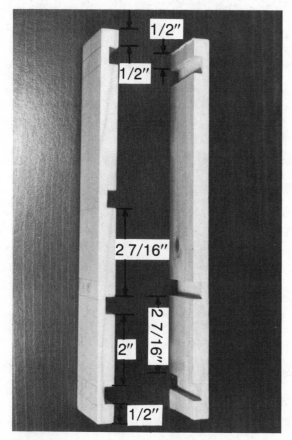

Fig. 6-34. The location of the dados cut into parts A, the top and bottom.

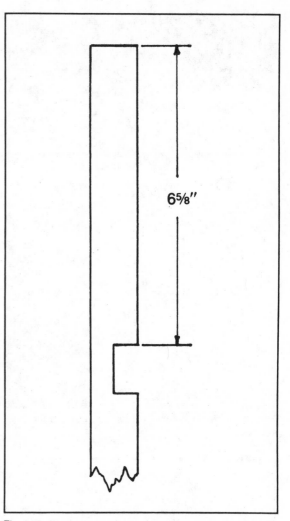

Fig. 6-35. There is a dado joint cut across both the sides 6⅝ inches down from the top end.

Table 6-7. Shadow-Box Clock Materials.

Part	Quantity	Size	Description
A	2	½″ × 2½″ × 11″	top & bottom
B	2	½″ × 2½″ × 17½″	sides
C	1	½″ × 2½″ × 9½″	horizontal supports
D	1	½″ × 2½″ × 10⅝″	vertical support
E	1	½″ × 2½″ × 5¼″	vertical support
F	1	½″ × 2½″ × 5″	right lower shelf
G	1	½″ × 2½″ × 3½″	left lower shelf
H	1	¼″ × 6⅜″ × 6⅛″	dial mounting board
I	2	½″ × 1⅝″ × 6½″	dial supports
	1	handshaft for ½″ thick dial	battery movement
	1		set of hands to fit

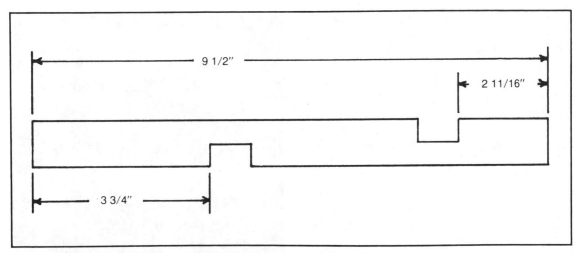

Fig. 6-36. There are two dados cut on part C, the horizontal support.

Fig. 6-37. Trial assemble the parts to ensure proper fit. The parts must be kept square.

Fig. 6-38. The vertical supports of the shadow-box clock in place.

The location of the dados on parts A can be found by following the dimensions shown in Fig. 6-34. Again, these dados are ½ inch wide and ¼ inch deep. There are dados also cut into both parts B. These are located 6⅝ inches down from the top end (Fig. 6-35).

There are only two more dados to be cut. These are located on part C. Part C is ½ of an inch thick, 2½ inches wide, and 9½ inches long. The first is cut on the bottom of the board, 3¾ inches from the left, the other, on the top, is 2 11/16 inches from the right (Fig. 6-36).

Cut part D (the upper vertical support). The size of this support is ½ inch thick, 2½ inches wide, and 10⅝ inches long.

Trial assemble the parts cut thus far to see if

Fig. 6-40. The left lower shelf fits between parts B and D.

Fig. 6-39. The right lower shelf is inserted between parts B and D, resting on part E.

they fit properly (Fig. 6-37). Once the pieces have been fitted, glue the box together; be sure to keep it square. Be careful to wipe any excess glue from the joints.

While the box assembly is drying, cut the remaining 2½-inch-wide pieces to the proper lengths.

There are two vertical dividers. The longest, part D, is 10⅝ inches long. Part E is 5¼ inches long. Part D is inserted between the dados cut in parts A and C. The other vertical divider is placed in the remaining dado in the bottom (as shown in Fig. 6-38).

There are two horizontal dividers that remain to be put into the shadow box case. Part F measures 5 inches long. It fits between parts B and D, resting on part E. See Fig. 6-39. To make sure the horizontal divider is not placed in crooked, measure 5 inches up along both parts B and D. This will be the location of the bottom of the horizontal divider. The other horizontal divider (part G) is placed between vertical part D and part B on the left side. This 3½-inch-long shelf has been glued in place 3⅜ inches up from the bottom; but it may be placed at any height. Possibly two shelves could be put into the space, dividing the large area into three smaller compartments (Fig. 6-40).

The large opening in the upper left corner is for the clock. Cut one piece of ¼-inch-thick plywood or Masonite to fit into the clock compartment, which is 6⅜ inches by 6⅛ inches. This will be the dial-mounting board. There are two mounting board supports, parts I, that measure ½ of an inch thick, 1⅝ inches wide, and 6⅛ inches long. Glue these supports in the clock movement compartment. One

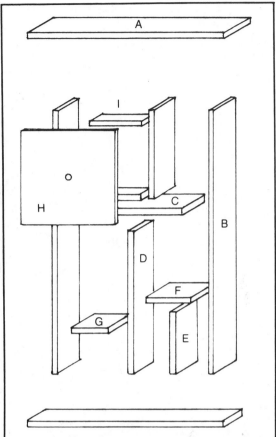

Fig. 6-42. Exploded view of the wooden parts that make up the shadow-box clock.

is glued to the top of the compartment and the other is glued to the bottom. Both parts I must be held flush with the back edge (Fig. 6-41). See also Fig. 6-42.

Drill a ⅜-inch-diameter hole through the center of the dial mounting board (part I). The center can be easily found by drawing a light pencil line diagonally from corner to corner, then another diagonal line from the other corners. Where the lines cross will be the center.

Glue the dial mounting board onto the dial supports previously glued into the clock compartment.

All of the wood parts for the shadow-box clock as described in this section have now been cut and glued into place. Each piece can be stained and

Fig. 6-41. The dial supports are glued flush with the back of the shadow box.

varnished, or any other type of finish can be applied. The dial used on this example is a white cardboard with a black timering, but any style of hour markers can be used.

This clock easily lends itself to mass production. Because all pieces are the same ½-inch thickness and 2½-inch width, many boards can be cut to these sizes and then cut to the proper lengths. The dados cut in some of the pieces can also be cut in mass.

The shadow box clock, although simple to build, is unusual yet functional. With its clean, straight lines, it is sure to be a welcome gift or a popular item at art sales.

MODERN SCHOOLHOUSE CLOCK

The modern schoolhouse clock (Fig. 6-43) is a

Fig. 6-44. Edge glue two 1½-inch-thick boards to form a 14¼-×-14¼-inch clock front.

Fig. 6-43. Modern schoolhouse clock.

blend of modern design and the traditional clock mechanism. The rounded, circular clock front—combined with the square box lines of the pendulum compartment—are all elements of modern style furniture. The gentle swing of the pendulum swaying in the pendulum compartment is a step back to yesteryear.

This is a project that cannot easily be built with hand tools alone. The circular clock face is made by turning the round shape on a wood lathe. The front can be cut and shaped with hand tools, but the process will be time consuming.

Begin by edge glueing two 1½-inch-thick boards together to form an area 14¼ inches wide and 14¼ inches long (as shown in Fig. 6-44). See Table 6-8. Once dried, set a point of a compass in the center and draw a 14-inch-diameter circle.

Drill the clock movement, hand-shaft hole through the board at the center of the circle. This hole is usually ⅜ of an inch, but check the movement that will be used.

Table 6-8. Modern Schoolhouse Clock Materials.

Part	Quantity	Size	Description
A	1	1½" × 14" × 14"	wood clock front
B	2	¾" × 2½" × 17½"	compartment sides
C	2	¾" × 2½" × 6"	compartment top & bottom
D	4	¾" × ¾" × 2¼"	corner blocks (pine)
E	1	½" × 1⅜" × 7½"	compartment trim vertical
F	2	½" × 2⅛" × 5"	compartment trim vertical
G	1	¼" × 6" × 16"	back
	3	1¼", number eight	flathead screws

With a band saw, sabre saw, or any other saw that can cut curves in thick wood, cut out the 14-inch diameter circle. It is advisable that the line previously drawn remain on the board—not cut off. Then file and sand down to the line.

Lay the dial, that will be used for the clock, on the front side of the 14-inch-diameter, wood-clock front. Center the dial by lining it up with the hand-shaft hole previously drilled in the wood clock front. When it is properly positioned, trace the outline of the dial (Fig. 6-45). Turn the wood clock front over and mount a lathe-face plate. While turning at a slow speed, true the roundness of the outside diameter and curve the sharp edge along the front edge of the wood disk (Fig. 6-46).

Carve out the diameter of the dial that has been traced. This should be carved to a depth of 1 inch,

Fig. 6-46. Round the outside edge of the wood clock front.

Fig. 6-45. Trace the outline of the clock dial on the wood clock front.

leaving a thickness of ½ inch. Frequently test fit the dial into the recess being carved to ensure that it is neither too large nor too small. When the recess is at a proper depth and diameter, curve the inside of the edge, creating a smooth gently flowing curve from the dial to the outside (Fig. 6-47). Sand the wood clock front while it is on the lathe. Also sand it when it is removed in order to remove any marks left from the lathe.

Cut the two sides of the pendulum compartment (parts B). These measure ¾ of an inch thick, 2½ inches wide, and 17½ inches long. Parts C, the pendulum box top and bottom, should also be cut. They are both ¾ of an inch thick, 2½ inches wide, and 6 inches long. These are glued between parts C, as shown in Fig. 6-48.

Fig. 6-47. The dial recess has been cut and the wood clock front rounded.

In each corner of the compartment, glue a ¾-inch-thick-by-¾-inch-wide, 2¼-inch-long corner block. These blocks (parts D) will be kept flush with the front edge of the compartment and should be ¼ of an inch in from the rear edge (Fig. 6-49).

Cut the ¼-inch-thick back. This can be made of either Masonite or plywood. The back (part G) measures 6 inches wide and 16 inches long. This has been designed to fit into the pendulum compartment, resting on the corner blocks. Test fit the back in the pendulum compartment, altering it as necessary to fit. This will be held in place by four ¾-inch-long, number-six flathead screws, screwed through the back into the corner blocks.

Remove the back temporarily and lay the pendulum compartment on the back of the wood clock front, part A (Fig. 6-50). The side of the compartment should be 3 inches from the center of the hand-shaft hole, and the top should be 3½ inches above the center of the hand shaft hole. While this is laying in the correct location, lightly trace around the portion of the pendulum compartment that is laying on the wood clock front—both inside and out.

Remove the pendulum compartment from the wood clock front. Drill three, ⅛-inch-holes through the wood clock front. The first of these holes is located 3¾ inches in from the outside line in the outline of the top (Fig. 6-51). The two other holes are 6 inches down from the top line (also centered between the lines). Through these holes, three 1¼ inches long, number eight flathead screws will be screwed through the wood clock front into the pendulum compartment.

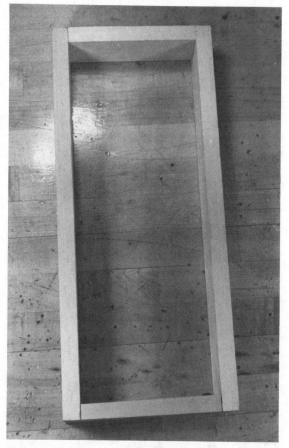

Fig. 6-48. The parts of the pendulum box glued together.

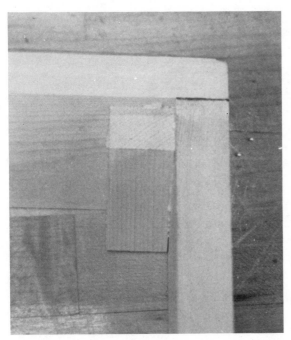

Fig. 6-49. The corner supports are flush with the front edge and ¼-inch back from the rear edge.

Fit the dial movement and pendulum into the clock compartment. This is a trial fit only. Now is the time for the craftsman to take a picture off the wall and hang the clock assembly. Take time to admire or criticize your work.

Well, enough self-evaluation. Back to work. Cut the two pendulum compartment trim pieces, parts E and F. Part E measures ½ of an inch thick, 1⅜ inches wide, and 7½ inches long. Part F is ½ inch thick, 2⅛ inches wide, and 5 inches long.

If the clock assembly hasn't yet been removed from the wall, do so now. Completely disassemble the clock. Lay the two-sided pendulum compartment trim pieces on the pendulum compartment in the position where they belong, as shown in Fig. 6-52. On top of this, lay the wood clock front in its correct position. Draw the outline of the wood clock front on the two trim pieces (Fig. 6-53). Cut and carefully sand the curves so they will fit neatly against the wood clock front. Lay part F, the bottom trim piece, on a flat surface. On this, lay the wood clock front as shown in Fig. 6-54. Trace the 14-inch-diameter curve from one corner to the other

(Fig. 6-55). Cut and sand the curve, and fit it between parts E.

When all the parts fit together correctly, glue the trim pieces to the pendulum compartment. Also glue and screw the wood clock front to the pendulum compartment (Figs. 6-56 and 6-57).

After allowing the clock cabinet assembly ample time to dry, sand the sides and bottom of the pendulum compartment to ensure that the trim pieces are flush with the compartment.

The modern schoolhouse clock is now completed, short of applying a finish. The finish can be a stain with varnish of any of the many materials currently available at any hardware store. When the finish is dry, install the dial, movement, and find it a place of honor. It will serve your needs for years to come.

Fig. 6-50. Lay the pendulum box on the wood clock front. Trace its outline.

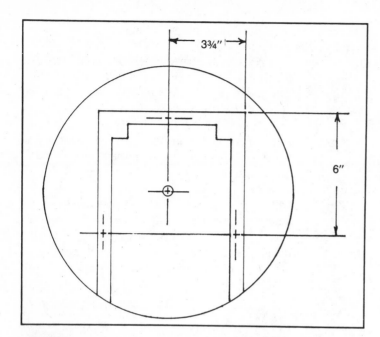

3¾"

6"

Fig. 6-51. Find the location of the three holes that will be drilled throught the wood clock front.

Fig. 6-52. The vertical pendulum compartment trim pieces in place.

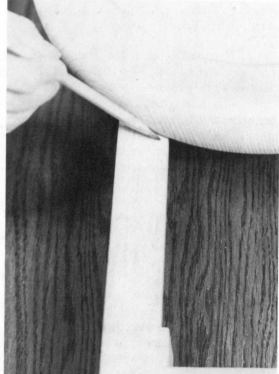

Fig. 6-53. Draw the curve of the wood clock front on the vertical trim boards.

Table 6-9. Modern Wall Clock Materials.

Quantity	Size	Description
1	¾″ × 11½″ × 16″	main clock face
2	¾″ × any size	outside supports
2	¾″ × any size	outside supports
1		battery clock movement
1		set of hands to fit movement
1		set of hour markers (optional)

Fig. 6-54. Draw the curve of the wood clock front on the horizontal trim board.

MODERN WALL CLOCK

The modern wall clock shown in Fig. 6-58 is an inexpensive project that can be made of wood scraps usually found in the shop. The design calls for three different types of wood, but it could easily be built with one type of wood, using various colored stains.

Modern or contemporary furniture is characterized by many straight lines, wood finished close to its natural color, and the use of contrasting colors. This clock meets all three requirements. The type of hour markers you choose to use will also emphasize its style.

The large center board for the clock face can be made any size, but a ¾-×-11½-×-16-inch board was used in this example. A piece of commercially cut 1-×-12-inch pine will measure ¾ × 11½ inches. See Table 6-9.

Fig. 6-55. The horizontal trim board with curve cut.

Fig. 6-56. Glue the trim boards to the pendulum compart-ment. Also screw the wood clock front onto the compartment.

Plane the top and bottom edges of the board if they are not already smooth. Make sure that each corner is square, resulting in a perfect rectangle.

The location of the center hole will have to be found so the hole can be drilled for the hand shaft. To find the center, draw a diagonal line from one corner down to the opposite corner, repeating this step for the other two corners. Where the two lines meet will mark the location of the center hole (Fig. 6-59).

An interesting effect you might want to try at this point is to move the hand-shaft hole to one side or the other or up or down. This will offset the clock face and give it informal balance that is often used in modern furniture. The space remaining will allow you to decorate the face in many ways. Decoupage a picture or favorite quote. Mount a favorite photo-

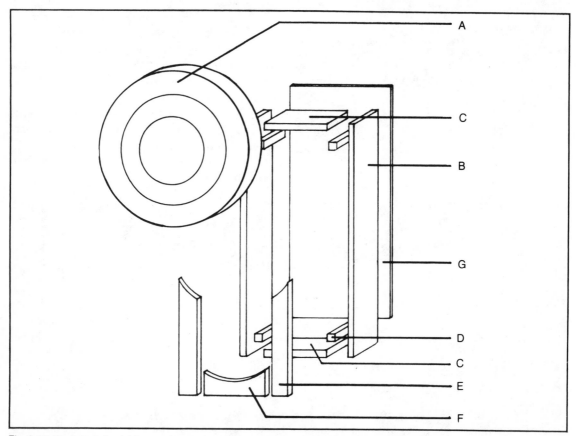

Fig. 6-57. Exploded view of the wood parts that make up the modern schoolhouse clock. (The movement and dial used on the example are courtesy of Klockit.)

104

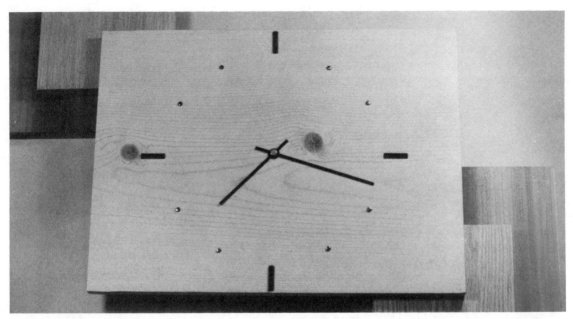

Fig. 6-58. Modern wall clock.

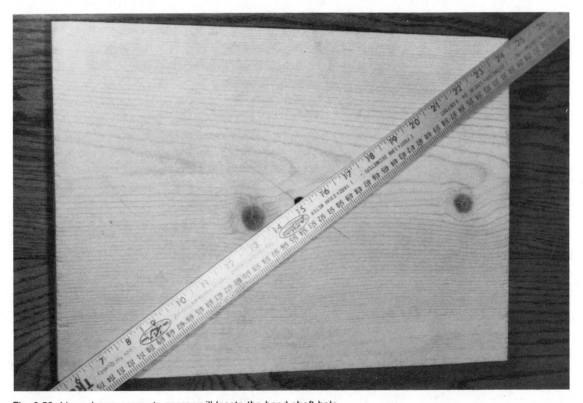

Fig. 6-59. Lines drawn corner to corner will locate the hand-shaft hole.

graph or simply apply a small bouquet of dried flowers.

When the center hand-shaft hole has been found, locate the positions of the hour markers. Instructions for this operation can be found in Chapter 3. Mark the hour marks by pounding a small nail into the wood at each point, and then remove the nail. The hole left will remain visible even after sanding; pencil marks are easily removed during such operations.

Sand the large center board to a smooth, scratch-free surface. This will be the focal point of the clock. Make sure that there are no distracting imperfections.

The decorative side panels can be cut any size and, for that matter, any shape. In this example, two pieces of dark wood (such as walnut or mahogany) measuring ½ × 2½ × 4½ inches were cut out and sanded, then glued and nailed (or screwed) to the back of the large center board. Make sure the nails or screws are long enough to reach through the ½-inch grid piece and into, but not through the center board. A ¾-inch wood screw with the head countersunk should work fine. The larger outer pieces were both cut from the same type of material. They can be made of light- or dark-colored wood. The lower left one is ¾ × 7¼ × 8½-inches and the other is ¾ × 5½ × 7¼ inches. If these sizes aren't available in your scrap wood pile, then virtually any size will do.

Before you glue these into place, you should cut two small, ½-inch scraps. These will be glued to the back of the large center board, out of sight. These will give more support to the larger pieces when they are glued and nailed in position (Figs. 6-60 aand 6-61). Thoroughly sand the parts before they are permanently attached to the clock.

If you have used two or three types of wood, you will only need to put a clear finish on the clock to show the contrasting colors of the woods. If you have built the entire project of one species of wood, you have a few alternatives. Each piece could be stained in another color to create a clock which demands attention. All pieces could be stained the same color to match or contrast the colors of the room or all pieces could be simply left natural in

Fig. 6-60. A scrap block the same thickness as parts B will provide support to parts C.

order to "weather." The moisture in the air will slowly cause the wood to take on a gray tone.

The type of hour markers used on this clock is limited only by the craftsman's imagination. There are some guidelines, however, that will help to keep it looking modern.

☐ The simpler the better.

☐ Small, petite markers will be better than large ones.

☐ Try to find a marker that will contrast with the color of the center board, but possibly match that of the outside boards.

☐ One-fourth inch holes drilled through at the hour markers will allow the viewer to see the color of the wall on which the clock is hung. This could also be considered modernistic.

Make sure the hands selected continue to emphasize the modern design. Generally, straight hands of medium to thin width are used in this style. The fancy scroll work found on many hands might

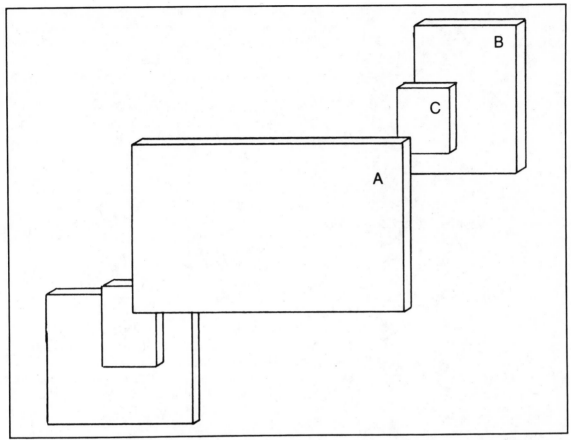

Fig. 6-61. Exploded view of the modern wall clock showing its wood parts. (The movement and hands used on this clock are courtesy of Klockit.)

not look good on this modernistic clock, yet possibly the contrast of styles is the effect desired.

COLONIAL WALL CLOCK

The true attributes of the colonial wall clock (Fig. 6-62) are its simplistic construction techniques highlighted by its graceful flowing lines. The shape of the clock front reflects an era past when life was calm, the pace was slow, and Colonial was the style. This classic style clock is made up of six basic component parts. The front is the most obvious part. The clock movement compartment is made of a top, bottom, two sides, and a back. The fact that there are so few parts demonstrates its ease of construction.

The clock movement compartment is the first section to be built. Begin by cutting the top and bottom (parts A and B). These should be ¾ of an inch thick, 2⅜ inches wide, and 6½ inches long. Also cut the two sides (parts C). These measure ¾ of an inch thick, 2⅜ inches wide, and 12 inches long. See Table 6-10.

The bottom (part B) will require a 1-×-3-inch hole cut out of it. This hole is where the pendulum shaft will extend through the clock movement compartment (Fig. 6-63). The hole will be located 1¾ inches in from the ends. The cutout should be large enough for most movements. In the event it is not large enough for the intended movement, it can be enlarged as required.

The four parts of the movement compartment are glued together. They can be reinforced with

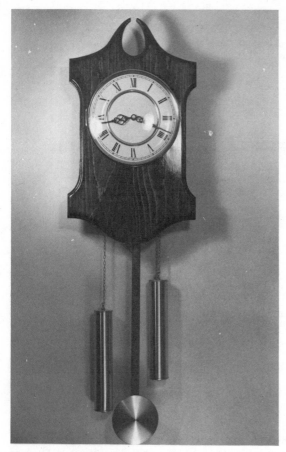

Fig. 6-62. Colonial wall clock.

drying, the clock front can be drawn and cut. The front is cut from a piece of wood ¾ of an inch thick, 11 inches wide, and 18½ inches long. Use the grid pattern in Fig. 6-67 to find the coordinates that plot the points for the outline of the clock front. It is necessary to draw only half of the clock front as shown on the grid pattern. Because the front is symmetrical (same on both sides of center), only one side needs to be drawn. It can then be turned over and drawn on the other side.

Cut the clock front shape out while being careful to leave the line on the wood. Using a file and sandpaper, smooth the edges and remove any blemishes that would detract from the clock's appearance. The clock in the photographs has had the outside edges routed with a decorative router bit. The routing is optional. The edges can be rounded with a file or left square. Drill the clock hand-shaft hole. The location for this hole is determined from the grid pattern (Fig. 6-67).

This clock has been designed to use a clock movement with a hand-shaft length to fit through the ¾-inch-thick clock front. In the event the movement selected has a shorter hand-shaft length, it will be necessary to remove, by router or hammer and chisel, enough material to allow the movement to properly fit (Fig. 6-68).

Assemble the clock movement compartment and the clock front. This is accomplished by laying the clock movement compartment on the back surface of the clock front (Fig. 6-69). Center the compartment on the clock back. Lightly draw a pencil line along the outside of the clock compartment. Draw a light line also along the inside (Fig. 6-70).

While the clock movement compartment is removed, drill a ⅛-inch diameter hole through the

nails, screws, or corner blocks. Because the compartment will not be subject to continued stress, the corner blocks have been chosen. The corner blocks measure ¾ inch thick, ¾ inch wide, and 2⅛ inches long. Glue the corner blocks to the ends of the top and bottom as shown in Fig. 6-64. They must be held flush with the ends of parts A and B, and also flush with the front edge (Fig. 6-64).

Part G, the mounting block, is ¾ inch thick, 1½ inches wide, and 4 inches long. It should be glued to part A, the top. Hold the mounting block flush with the edge of part A, as in Fig. 6-65.

After allowing the glue to set, glue the two sides to the top and bottom. Clamp this assembly and allow it ample time to thoroughly set (Fig. 6-66).

While the clock movement compartment is

Table 6-10. Colonial Wall Clock Materials.

Part	Quantity	Size	Description
A	1	¾″ × 2⅜″ × 6½″	cabinet top
B	1	¾″ × 2⅜″ × 6½″	cabinet bottom
C	2	¾″ × 2⅜″ × 12″	cabinet sides
D	4	¾″ × ¾″ × 2⅛″	corner supports
E	1	¼″ × 6½″ × 10½″	back
F	1	¾″ × 11″ × 18½″	clock front
G	1	¾″ × 1½″ × 4″	mounting block
	4	¾″, number six	flathead screws

Fig. 6-63. The bottom of the clock movement compartment (part B) requires a 1-inch-wide-by-3-inch-long, pendulum-shaft hole.

Fig. 6-64. Glue corner blocks to the ends of the top and bottom, parts A and B.

Fig. 6-65. Glue a mounting block (part G) to the top (part A). The mounting block must be kept flush with the edge that will be glued against the clock front.

corner blocks. Cut the back to 6½ inches wide by 10½ inches long. Lay it into the compartment to check for fit. While it is laying in place, drill a 3/16-inch hole through the back and only ¼-inch into the four corner blocks. Turn four ¾-inch long, number-six flathead screws into the back holding it to the compartment.

The clock cabinet is now assembled except for the installation of the movement, dial, and bezel. The clock photographed includes the addition of decorative weight shells hanging from the rear of the clock. These shells are not essential to the operation of this particular movement, but the style the weight shells provide was the desired appearance. These were hung by drilling two ½-inch holes 1¾ inches from each end and 1½ inches from the

Fig. 6-66. The top and bottom are glued between the sides.

approximate center of the mounting block (Fig. 6-71). Apply a layer of glue to the movement compartment and also to the back side only of the clock front (between the pencil outlines).

Lay the movement compartment on the back in position. Turn a 1¼-inch, number-eight roundhead screw through the mounting block into the back of the clock front. Apply a weight to the clock movement compartment. This will act as a clamp while the glue is setting. The glue should be all that is required to hold the compartment to the clock front, but the screw has been added for extra strength. Allow the assembly ample time to dry before proceeding to the next step.

There is a ¼-inch-thick back that is screwed to the clock movement compartment back. The back is cut to fit into the compartment, resting on the

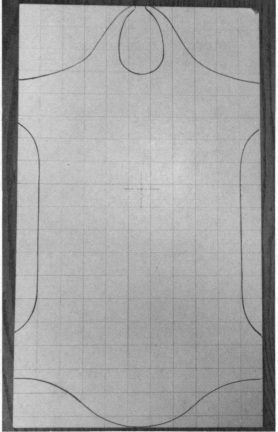

Fig. 6-67. The grid pattern of the colonial wall clock. Each square equals 1 inch.

Fig. 6-68. The rear of the colonial wall clock front has had some material removed to allow the movement hand-shaft to extend through.

Shaker-style clock that is described later in this chapter. They are alike in that they both have a certain simplicity in their design and carry the clean functional lines in the true Shaker tradition. The pendulum box clock does not require the complex cabinet door construction and the installation of glass panels.

The pendulum box clock has been designed to be made of pine wood because it is readily available at any local lumberyard, but any species of wood can be used. The size of this clock cabinet dictates the use of a movement with a 12- to 13-inch pendulum. If a movement with a pendulum length greater or less than this is used, it will be necessary to adjust the length of the sides and front accordingly. For example, if the pendulum length is increased by

clock front (Figs. 6-72 and 6-73). Inside the clock movement compartment, screw two ¾-inch, number-six screws, particularly into the sides, about 2 inches above the ½-inch holes. The chain for the weight shells will hang from these screws.

The clock that results from these instructions is sure to be an inexpensive, attractive one that will be appreciated by anyone who receives it. This is also an excellent clock for producing for resale because it involves few wood parts and contains a commercially produced dial and bezel. This reduces the time of construction.

PENDULUM BOX CLOCK

The clock shown in Fig. 6-74 is similar to the large

Fig. 6-69. Lay the movement compartment on the clock front to draw its outline.

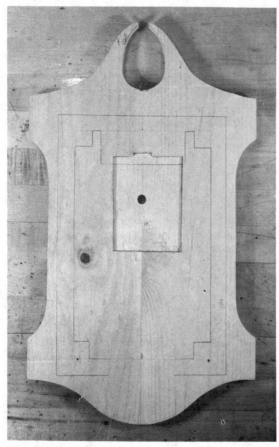

Fig. 6-70. The outline of the compartment on the rear surface of the clock front.

Fig. 6-71. Drill a ⅛-inch hole through the mounting block.

Fig. 6-72. If weight shells will be used on the colonial wall clock, two ½-inch holes should be drilled on the movement compartment bottom.

3 inches, the clock cabinet will need to be increased the same amount. The front and sides will have to be 25¾ inches long, and not the 22¾-inch length as described in these instructions.

Begin construction by cutting the two sides (part A and B) and the front (part F). The sides measure ¾ of an inch thick, 4⅛ inches wide, and 22¾ inches long. The front is made of a single piece of wood. Because it is the focal point of the clock, it should be free from defects and have a pleasing grain pattern. The front measures ¾ × 10¾ × 22¾ inches. See Table 6-11.

On the front, measure down from the top 5½ inches and over from the side 5⅜ inches (Fig. 6-75). This is the center of the 7-inch dial cutout. Draw a 7-inch circle with a compass around this point. This

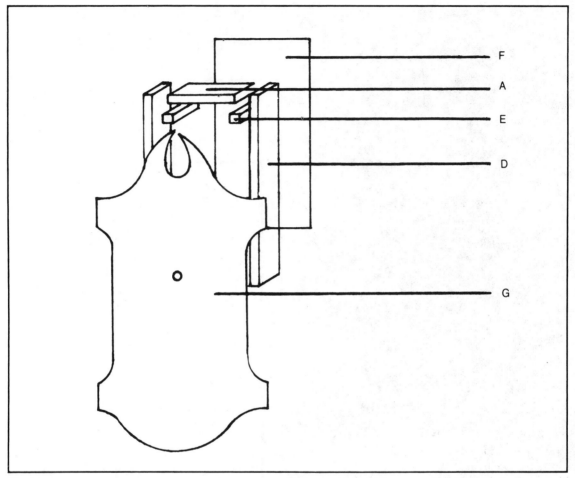

Fig. 6-73. An exploded view of the colonial wall clock. (The movement, dial, and hardware used on this clock are courtesy of Klockit.)

clock has been designed to use a 7½-inch-diameter round dial. If another size dial is to be used, adjustments will have to be made accordingly.

To find the location of the lower pendulum window, measure up from the bottom 2½ inches and draw a light pencil line. From the 2½-inch line, measure up 8¼ inches. From each side measure in 2⅜ inches. Draw a line at these points. This series of lines forms the outline for the pendulum window. The corners of the window can remain square or they can be rounded. This example used a 3-inch radius to mark the rounded corners (Fig. 6-75). Cut out the pendulum window; take care not to cut outside the line into the material that will remain.

Table 6-11. Pendulum-Box Clock Materials.

Part	Quantity	Size	Description
A	1	¾" × 4⅛" × 22¾"	side
B	1	¾" × 4⅛" × 22¾"	side
C	1	¾" × 5⅜" × 11⅞"	top
D	1	¾" × 5⅜" × 11⅞"	bottom
E	8	¾" × ¾" × 4"	support blocks
F	1	¾" × 10¾" × 22¾"	front
G	1	¼" × 9" × 9"	dial mounting board (plywood)
H	1	⅛" × 9¼" × 22¾"	back (plywood/masonite)
	32	1¼", number six	roundhead screws
	8	¾", number eight	roundhead screws
	1	12" pendulum	battery or windup movement
	1	7½" diameter	round dial
	1		set of hands sized to fit

Fig. 6-74. Pendulum box clock.

Parts A (right side) B (left side), C (top), D (bottom), and F (front) are now cut to size. Next cut the six ¾-inch-thick-¾-inch-wide-by-4-inches long support blocks (parts E).

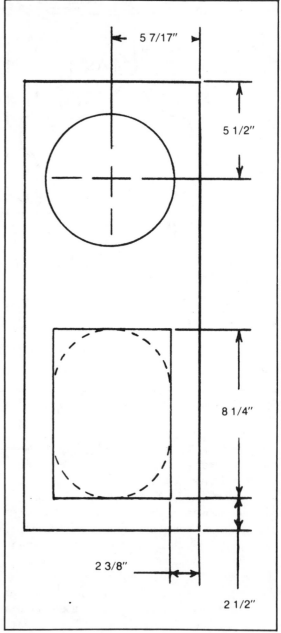

5 7/17″

5 1/2″

8 1/4″

2 3/8″

2 1/2″

Fig. 6-75. The drawing indicates the location of the dial center and the pendulum bob window.

Both the dial hole and the pendulum window of the example have been given a curved edge. This was done by using a rounding over router bit for the dial hole and a cove bit to form the design on the lower hole. If you do not have access to these router bits, almost any bit that cuts a decorative edge will work. If you do not have use of a router, you can still create an attractive edge on both of the holes by rounding the edge with a file, and then sanding it smooth with medium and then fine sandpaper.

Cut the top (C) and bottom (D) to the same size, ¾ inch thick, 5 3/7 inches wide, and 11⅞ inches long. These are given an edge treatment similar to that on the clock front (Fig. 6-76). Three of the edges are curved or routed. The example has the edges routed with the same bit as was used on the pendulum window.

Fig. 6-76. The top and bottom parts (C and D) have two ends and one edge routed or rounded.

Fig. 6-78. Two support blocks are located on the inside edges of part F. Two others are glued at the top and bottom of the front.

Two 3/16-inch-screw-pilot holes must be drilled through one side of each support block and two others through the adjacent side (Fig. 6-77).

The next operation takes place on the back of part F, the front piece. Draw line ¾ of an inch in from both edges. This is where the two ¾-inch-thick sides will meet the front. Glue and screw two of the support blocks 7¼ inches up from the bottom and along the ¾-inch line previously drawn (Fig. 6-78). Use 1 ¼-inch long, number-six roundhead screws. Also screw and glue two of the support blocks on the top and bottom of part F (the front). These should be flush with the top and bottom edges and 3 ⅜ inches in from the sides (Fig. 6-78). Allow this assembly to dry.

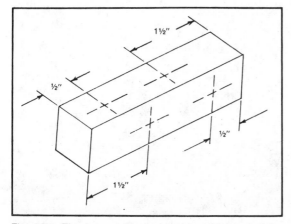

Fig. 6-77. The support blocks have two 3/16-inch holes drilled through the top and two through the side.

It is now necessary to glue and screw a support block on the inside of parts A and B (the sides). The support blocks should be positioned even with the top and bottom. Make sure the blocks are kept flush with the front edge as well as the top and bottom. An easy way to screw these into position is to glue and clamp them into position while you put the screws in.

If all parts have been cut to the correct size, the support block will lay flush with the front edge of the side, and it will be 1/8 of an inch in from the back edge (Fig. 6-79).

Apply a layer of glue to the front edges of the side pieces and also to the support blocks. The 1 ¼-inch, number-six roundhead screws should

Fig. 6-79. Support blocks glued to the sides must be mounted flush with the ends and the front edge, leaving ⅛ inch at the rear edge.

to thoroughly dry before any other work on it is done.

While the cabinet is drying, cut the ¼-inch-thick dial mounting board. This is cut 9 inches wide and 9 inches long. It is necessary to locate and drill the 3/8-inch, hand-shaft hole in the center. Find the center point by drawing a diagonal line from the upper left corner to the lower right corner and a line from the upper right corner down to the lower left corner.

How the dial is attached to the dial-mounting board is determined by the type of dial intended for use. Some metal dials come with predrilled holes and tiny nails or screws to hold the dial in place. If this is the case, all that is necessary is to align the hand-shaft hole on the dial with the hand-shaft hole on the mounting board.

Fig. 6-80. The mounting blocks that are attached to the clock front are used to connect the sides to the front.

be used to screw and glue the front and sides together (Fig. 6-80). Don't rely on the screws alone to apply pressure on the front. Also use clamps. If there are not any clamps available it is a simple matter to lay a board over the two sides and place a heavy weight (such as a cement block) on it. This assembly should be allowed to dry over night before the next step.

Again using the 1 ¼ -inch, number-six round-head screws, glue and screw the clock case assembly to the top and bottom pieces. The back of parts (B and C) should be even with the back of the top and bottom (Fig. 6-81).

Give the finished clock cabinet a final sanding. Then stain or varnish. Again allow the clock cabinet

Fig. 6-81. Affix the bottom and top to the cabinet assembly.

the movement on one side of the mounting board and the dial on the other, the washer and nut can be tightened to hold the three parts together (Fig. 6-82).

To fasten the dial mounting board to the clock cabinet, it is first necessary to drill four 3/16-inch holes at the four corners of the mounting board. These holes are drilled 1 inch in from the sides and 1 inch in from the top and bottom (Fig. 6-83). Screw the dial mounting board to the clock cabinet using the four ¾-inch, number-eight roundhead screws. Care must be taken to correctly line up the dial in the dial hole of the clock front.

At this point, it is hard to resist the urge to assemble the clock movement and cabinet to see how it looks. Go ahead. It's a great time to make sure everything fits together properly. Besides, it's

Fig. 6-82. Most dials can be mounted to the dial-mounting board by the clock hand-shaft nut, holding it in place.

If a dial printed on paper or cardboard is to be used, it is best to use rubber cement to hold the dial to the mounting board. Be sure to try the glue on a spot on the dial that won't show just in case the glue damages the paper. Because rubber cement is a contact glue, it is necessary to apply a layer of cement to both the dial and the mounting board. Then allow them to dry before putting them together. There is a possible problem with this method. When the dial is placed on the mounting board, it is necessary that both parts be lined up exactly; once they touch each other they won't be able to be pulled apart without damaging the paper dial.

If a metal or ceramic dial is to be used, the hand-shaft can be used to hold the dial in place. With

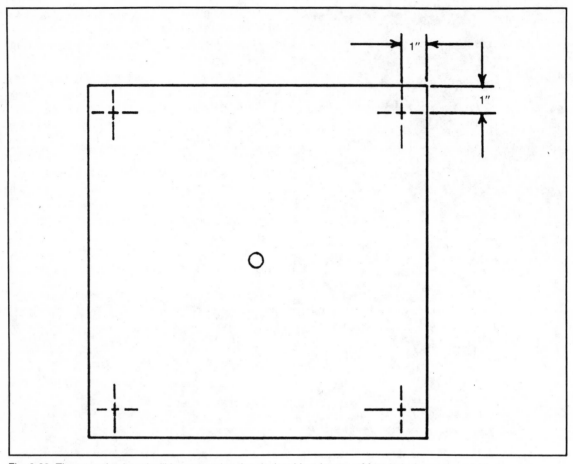

Fig. 6-83. The mounting board will be screwed to the clock cabinet by use of four ⅜-inch, number-eight screws.

fun to look at your work!

The back (part H) is made of ⅛-inch-thick Masonite. It measures 9¼ inches by 22¾ inches. This has been designed to fit between the side walls of the cabinet (being held in place by four ¾ inch, number-eight roundhead screws). These screws must be placed ⅜ of an inch in from the sides and ⅜ of an inch from the top and bottom (Figs. 6-84 and 6-85). Placement of the screws at these points will permit you to screw them into the ends of the support blocks. Do not glue the back to the cabinet. It will be necessary from time to time to remove it to change the batteries or make repairs to the movement.

The front side of part H (the back) is painted flat black on the example. This will provide a background that will draw attention to the pendulum when viewed from the front.

The pendulum box clock cabinet is now complete. All that remains is to apply some type of finish. The type to use can only be determined by the craftsman. You might want to stain the wood then varnish or just varnish the cabinet. Another option is to use one of the oil finishes available at most hardware stores. Whichever type you choose, don't rush through this step. Read directions and take your time. A beautiful piece of woodworking can be reduced to kindling wood if the finish is poorly applied.

The pendulum box clock is a very attractive and appealing clock. It is relatively simple and inexpensive to build. It is also an excellent clock for

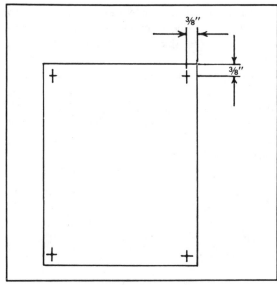

Fig. 6-84. The back is screwed into the four mounting blocks of the clock cabinet assembly.

the craftsman who builds for resale and a great clock for gift giving. It shows the person receiving the gift how much you care when you give them a gift you have created.

THE SUPERIOR

The superior (Fig. 6-86) is a large, impressive clock not requiring much wood to build. In fact, the entire clock can be built from a 1-×-6-×-6-foot piece of pine and another that measures 1 × 10 × 4 feet. See Table 6-12. It is not necessary to build with pine. Any wood will do, providing a straight, knot-free 24-inch length can be obtained for the four corner posts.

Construction on the superior begins by cutting the two parts A. These will be ¾ of an inch thick, 5½ inches wide, and 11½ inches long. These, and all other parts, must be cut with square corners.

Clamp the two boards together as shown in

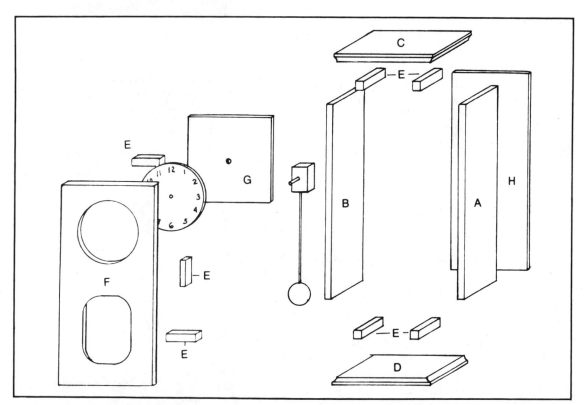

Fig. 6-85. Exploded view of the pendulum box clock showing the component wooden parts. (The movement and dial are courtesy of Klockit.)

Table 6-12. Superior Clock Materials.

Part	Quantity	Size	Description
A	2	3/4″ × 5 1/2″ × 11 1/2″	top and bottom
B	4	3/4″ × 3/4″ × 23 1/4″	corner posts
C	8	each 2 inches	3/8″ dowel
D	2	3/4″ × 3 7/8″ × 8 1/4″	first trim board
E	2	3/4″ × 2 5/8″ × 6″	final trim board
F	2	3/4″ × 6 5/8″ × 6 5/8″	cylinder body
G	2	3/4″ × 6 5/8″ × 6 5/8″	cylinder body
H	1	3/4″ × 6 5/8″ × 6 5/8″	cylinder back
I	1	1/4″ × 6 5/8″ × 6 5/8″	cylinder front
	1	7″ diameter	dial
	2	3/16″ × 3 1/2″	screws
	3	3/4″, number six	flathead wood screws
	1	16″ pendulum	battery movement

Fig. 6-87. Both boards will have four ⅜-inch diameter holes drilled in them. It is necessary that the holes be drilled at the exact location on both boards. If the two boards are clamped together while being drilled, the holes in the bottom board cannot help but be in the exact location of the holes on the top.

Lay out the location of the ⅜-inch holes as they are shown in Fig. 6-88. This layout procedure need only be done on one of the two boards because they are clamped together. Drill the holes slowly. If the holes are drilled too quickly by exerting too much pressure, the drill bit will break through the bottom board—chipping the bottom surface. As the drill bit nears the end of the hole, reduce the pressure on the drill so that the bit will cut through—not break through.

The next operation will be to cut the four ¾-inch-thick-¾-inch-wide-and-23¾-inch-long corner posts (parts B). Carefully select the wood for these parts. They need to be straight and free from warp and knots. Look for a piece of wood that has a straight grain pattern rather than a grain pattern that curves. The curved grain could cause the thin, ¾-inch-square corner posts to warp. That would greatly detract from the fine lines of this clock.

On both ends of the four corner posts, draw diagonal lines from corner to corner. Where the two lines cross, drill a ⅜-inch diameter hole 1-inch deep (Fig. 6-89). Do this carefully so that the holes will be straight. Repeat this operation on both ends of the four corner posts.

Sand the corner posts and parts A prior to assembly. It will be much easier to sand the individual parts rather than the cabinet once it has been put together.

Cut eight lengths of ⅜-inch-diameter dowel. These should be 2 inches long. One end of each dowel should be chamfered as in Fig. 6-90. The chamfer can be done by rubbing the dowel against coarse sandpaper or by placing the dowel in a pencil sharpener and "sharpening" the dowel only slightly. This operation is rough on the pencil sharpener.

The chamfer is cut on the dowel end that will be inserted through the holes in part A, and into the holes drilled in the ends of parts B. If the dowel is chamfered, it will tend to slide into the hole easier—and the glue at the bottom of the hole will

Fig. 6-86. The superior clock.

Fig. 6-87. Clamp the two parts B together so that the four ⅜-inch holes will be drilled in both boards at the same time.

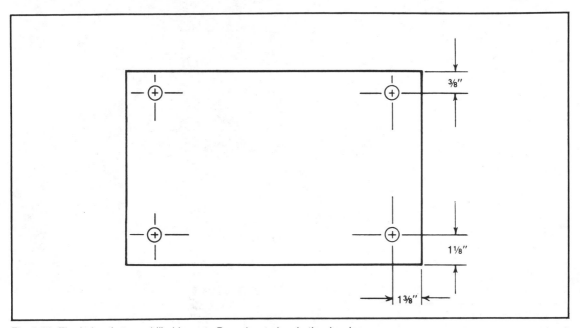

Fig. 6-88. The holes that are drilled in parts B are located as in the drawing.

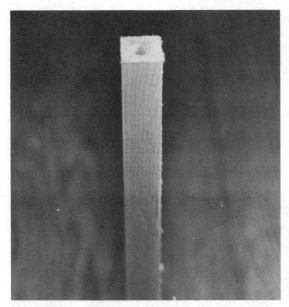

Fig. 6-89. The ends of parts E, the corner posts, require a ⅜-inch-diameter hole 1 inch deep in the center.

Fig. 6-91. Assembling the main portion of the cabinet with dowels.

slide up and around the dowel—thus providing a better grip.

Assemble the two parts A to the four corner posts (parts B). Be sure to place a small amount of glue into the hole and also on the dowel. Too much glue will not allow the dowel to penetrate deep enough into the hole. Gently tap the dowels into the holes. Striking the dowels with too much force

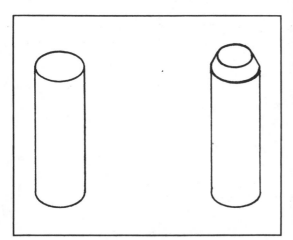

Fig. 6-90. One end of the ⅜-inch dowels should be chamfered to allow for stronger gluing.

Fig. 6-92. The corner posts must be kept square with the top and bottom. Clamps are required to hold the unit square while the glue dries.

Fig. 6-93. Carefully cut the portion of the dowel that projects above the surface of parts B.

could cause it to break off before reaching its full working depth (Fig. 6-91).

Before the glue has had a chance to dry, check to see that the corner posts and parts A are square (Fig. 6-92).

After allowing the glued-up assembly time to thoroughly dry, saw off the part of the dowel that is above the board (Fig. 6-93). Do this carefully so that the saw doesn't scratch the wood surface. A coarse piece of sandpaper wrapped around a wood block should be used to sand the dowels flush with the surface of the top and bottom boards.

The clock movement case for this clock is hung from the top (the upper part A) by two 3/16-×-3 ½-inch screws. Therefore, two additional holes will need to be drilled through the upper board. The 3/16-inch-diameter holes should be drilled through the board. Locate the positions of these holes as shown in Fig. 6-94. Countersink the holes so that the heads of the screws will be below the surface of part A. These holes are not to be drilled through the bottom board—only the top.

The front and ends of parts A must be rounded. This can be accomplished with a rasp and file, then sanded smooth, or with a router equipped with a rounding over bit or any decorative bit (Fig. 6-95). Rout only the front and two ends. The back edge is not rounded. Repeat the rounding process on the lower part A.

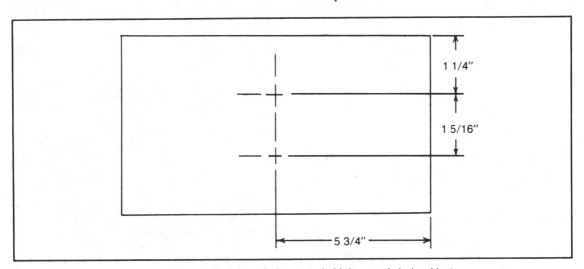

Fig. 6-94. The locations of the two holes drilled through the top to hold the round clock cabinet.

Fig. 6-95. The top and bottom can be routed or rounded over with a file.

glued to part D, but do not glue it to the upper part A. The screws that hold the clock movement cylinder must be inserted through the upper part A before parts A and D are glued on (Fig. 6-96).

Set aside the clock case assembly and allow it to dry. Do not glue part A onto the assembly. That will not be done until later in the process.

Cut out parts F, G, and H. These parts are circular in shape, with a diameter of 6⅝ inches. Do not finish sand these five disks; that step will come later. Part H will remain just as it is, but the two parts G and two parts F will require further work. The center of each will have a 5¾-inch-diameter circle removed from them (Fig. 6-97). The two parts F will have a cutout removed from the bottom of the circle (as can be seen in Fig. 6-98).

Fig. 6-96. Each decorative trim board must be aligned in the center of each preceding board.

There are four decorative trim boards that are glued to the top and bottom boards. Parts D are the first to be glued to the top and bottom. They measure ¾ of an inch thick, 3⅞ inches wide, and 8¼ inches long. The third and final trim boards are two parts E. Both of these are ¾ of an inch thick, 2⅝ inches wide, and 6 inches long.

Each of these pieces require the same router bit used earlier to rout the two ends and front edge. Once routed, sand all surfaces of the clock cabinet prior to gluing the parts to the bottom and the top. After the two parts are fixed to the bottom, it is difficult to properly sand the parts.

Carefully align and glue the bottom of part E (the final trim board) to part D. Then glue parts D and E to the lower part A. The top part E can be

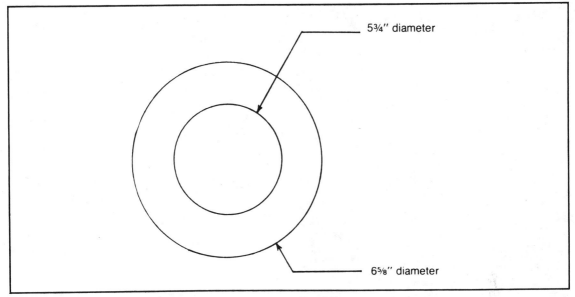

Fig. 6-97. There is a 5¾-inch circle cutout of four disks, parts E and F.

There is not a size given for the cutout on the parts F, because clock movements differ. The pendulum shaft will pass through the cutouts. Room must be provided so the sides will not interfere with the operation of the pendulum.

The next two sections (parts G) do not require the cutout as in parts F. These two will only have the 5¾-inch hole cut out of the center (Fig. 6-99).

The five disks form the clock movement case. They are to be glued together in the following

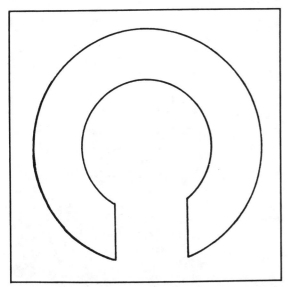

Fig. 6-98. The two parts E require a cutout to be removed from the bottom. When assembled, the clock movement pendulum-shaft will extend through the opening.

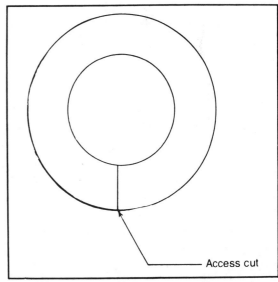

Fig. 6-99. The two center disks only have the 5¾-inch circle cut out of the center.

Fig. 6-100. The five disks that make up the clock movement cylinder are glued together with parts E on one end, and part G closes the back end.

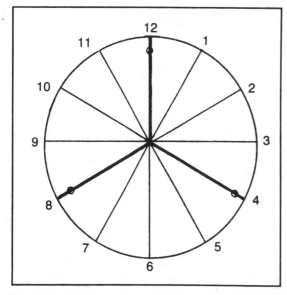

Fig. 6-101. The ¼-inch-thick cylinder front has a ⅜-inch hole drilled through the center and three ⅛-inch holes drilled at the 12, 4, and 8 positions of a clock dial.

manner. The two parts F are glued together, which are glued to the two parts G, and finally, part H is glued to the others (Fig. 6-100).

Cut the ¼-inch thick, 6⅝-inch-diameter part I. This part will not have its center cut out as the others. It will have a ⅜-inch hole drilled through its center. The clock movement hand shaft will project through this hole. Also drilled through this piece will be three ⅛-inch diameter holes. These holes are drilled ½ of an inch in from the outside edge and in the approximate locations of the 12, 4, and 8 on a clock dial (Fig. 6-101).

The three holes will need to be countersunk for the heads of three ¾-inch, number-six flathead screws. Screw part I, the ¼-inch-thick dial mounting board, onto the clock movement case, made up of parts F, G, and I. While this assembly is together, file and sand the 6⅝-inch cylinder down to the finished size of 6½ inches in diameter.

Along the top of the cylinder, opposite the

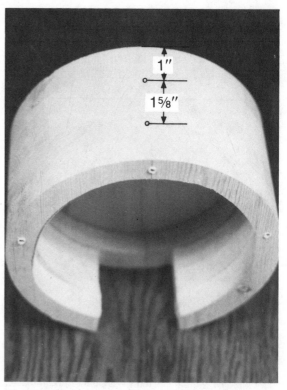

Fig. 6-102. The movement cylinder will have two holes drilled in the top. These holes are used to hang the cylinder.

pendulum cutout, drill two 3/16-inch holes. The first hole should be 1 inch in from the back, and the other will be located 1⅝ inches beyond the first (Fig. 6-102). These holes correspond to the holes previously drilled in the top of the cabinet.

All of the parts for this clock have now been cut, shaped, and sanded. It would be wise to stain and varnish all of the parts prior to assembly.

With the ¼-inch front of the movement cylinder removed, insert the hanging screws and place the nuts on the inside (Figs. 6-103 and 6-104). A thin-walled brass tube, such as those used as fuel lines on flying model airplanes, can be placed over the exposed threads of the screws.

The hand shaft of the movement is inserted through the ⅜-inch hole in the center of the ¼-inch cylinder front. The ¼-inch front is then screwed into place on the cylinder. The dial is held in place on the movement cylinder by the hand-shaft washer and nut.

The superior, as its name indicates, is a clock large in size with a commanding appearance. This clock, with its clean, neat design, will prove to be an enchanting conversation piece to all who gaze on its beauty.

SCHOOLHOUSE CLOCK

There are few clocks in America's past that involve more nostalgia than the traditional schoolhouse clock (Fig. 6-105). Its octagon wood front and pendulum cabinet remain the constant design of schoolhouse clocks; yet each craftsman who designs this style of clock has added just a little of himself to make the design his own.

This clock has been designed, as all clocks in this book, with ease of construction as its major

Fig. 6-103. The screws hanging down from the top (part A) are inserted into the holes previously drilled in the movement cylinder.

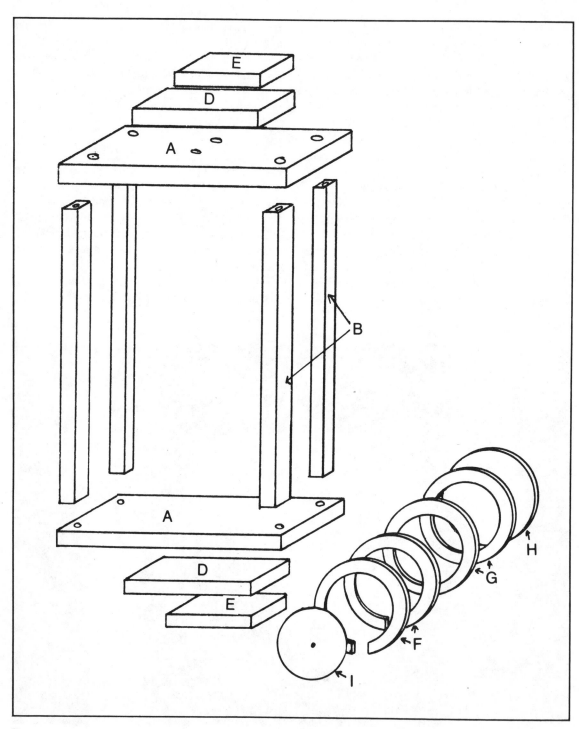

Fig. 6-104. An exploded view of the wood parts which make up the superior. The movement and dial used in this clock have been provided courtesy of Klockit.

128

Fig. 6-105. Schoolhouse clock.

Table 6-13. Schoolhouse Clock Materials.

Part	Quantity	Size	Description
A	1	¾" × 14" × 14"	octagon front
B	1	¼" × 6½" diameter	dial mounting board
C	2	¾" × 2½" × 18⅝"	cabinet sides
D	1	¾" × 2½" × 5¾"	cabinet top
E	1	¾" × 2" × 5¾"	cabinet bottom
F	2	¾" × ¾" × 2¼"	top corner block
G	2	¾" × ¾" × 1¾"	bottom corner block
H	1	½" × 7¼" × 9½"	pendulum cabinet front
I	1	¼" × 5¾" × 17⅛"	cabinet back
	3	½", number six	flathead screws
	3	1½", number eight	flathead screws
	1	12 to 14 inch	pendulum length movement hand shaft length for 5/16" thick dial
	1	9½" diameter	clock dial
	1		clock bezel to fit

eight edges of the octagon.

Locate the center of the octagon as shown in Fig. 6-107. At this point, draw a 6½-inch-diameter circle. Cut the circle out (Fig. 6-108). Using a router with a ½-inch-rabbeting bit, cut a ¼-inch-

consideration. Nevertheless, the style still retains the look and charm of its earlier counterparts.

Construction begins by securing a piece of wood ¾ of an inch thick, 14 inches wide, and 14 inches long. This will be part A, the octagon front. A board 14 inches wide is normally not available. If one can be found, it will be subject to warping. To reduce the possibility of warping, the 14-inch-wide board is best made up of two or more boards edge glued together (Fig. 6-106). See Table 6-13.

While the octagon front board is drying, draw the octagon shape on a piece of cardboard. The shape can be drawn by following the dimensions shown in Fig. 6-107. Cut out the cardboard templet and trace it on the wood octagon front. Cut the octagon shape out, taking care not to cut into the octagon shape. Then carefully file and sand the

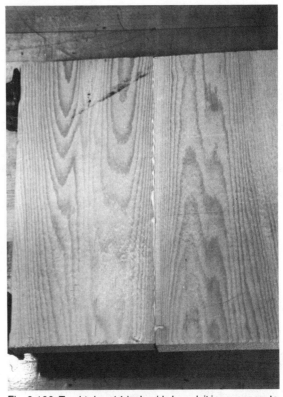

Fig. 6-106. To obtain a 14-inch-wide board, it is necessary to edge glue two boards together.

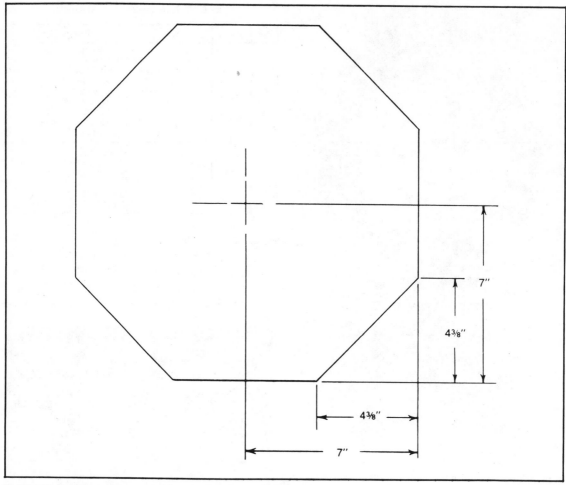

Fig. 6-107. How the octagon wood front is drawn on the cardboard templet.

deep rabbet around the inside of the 6½-inch circle cut (Fig. 6-104).

Part B, the ¼-inch-thick, 6½-inch-diameter disk has a ⅜-inch-diameter hole drilled through the center. Then it is fitted into the rabbet previously routed in the octagon board. Use three ½-inch, number-six screws to secure the disk in place (Fig. 6-110). Make sure the disk lies flush with the octagon front. If it is raised, it will interfere with the dial.

The movement and cabinet case is the next to be built. Cut the two parts C, the sides that measure ¾ of an inch thick, 2½ inches wide, and 18⅝ inches long. There will be a cutout made on the front edge

of each of these pieces. Measure 8¾ inches up from the bottom end and ½ inch in from the front edge (Fig. 6-111). Remove the ½-inch-×-8¾-inch section on both pieces.

Cut part D (the top) and part E (the bottom). They are both ¾ of an inch thick and 5¾ inches long. The width of the two differ. Part D is 2½ inches wide, while the bottom, part E, is 2 inches wide. These two pieces fit in between the sides as shown in Fig. 6-112.

Cut the corner blocks for the top corners. These will be glued in place to provide added strength for the cabinet. The top blocks (part F) are ¾ of an inch thick, ¾ of an inch wide, and 2¼ inches

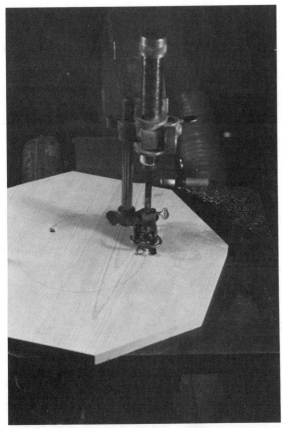

Fig. 6-108. Cut a 6½-inch diameter center out of the octagon front.

Fig. 6-109. Rout a ¼-inch deep, ½-inch-wide rabbet along the 6½-inch diameter center cutout.

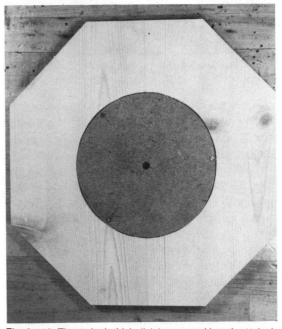

Fig. 6-110. The ¼-inch-thick disk is screwed into the ¼-inch deep, ½-inch-wide rabbet in the octagon clock front.

long. Make sure the corner blocks are kept ¼ of an inch from the back edge and flush with the front edge. The bottom corner blocks (G) are the same thickness and width, but they are 1¾ inches long. As with the top blocks, glue these in place ¼ of an inch in from the rear edge.

The pendulum cabinet front (part H) is the next part to be made. It measures ½ of an inch thick, 7¼ inches wide, and 9½ inches long. In this part, there is a pendulum window cut. The window can be of any shape the craftsman prefers. In this example an oval was cut, but a circle, square, or anything else may be used. Whatever the shape, the important consideration is that the center of the window be at the same point as the center of the pendulum bob.

On the bottom end of the pendulum cabinet front, there is a slight design cut. The shape of this

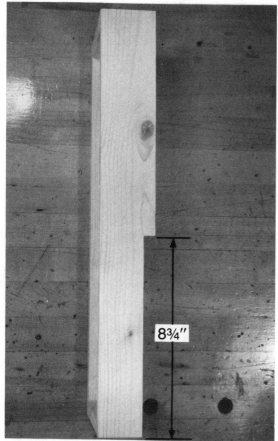

Fig. 6-111. The sides of the schoolhouse clock cabinet have a ½-×-8¾-inch recess cut away.

clock front.

On the rear octagon clock front, find the location of the screw holes that hold the clock front to the pendulum cabinet. The screw hole positions are located as shown in Fig. 6-115.

Drill the screw holes with a 3/16-inch drill bit. On the front of the octagon, the screw holes must be countersunk so that the heads of the flathead wood screws will be recessed below the surface of the clock front. With the octagon clock front laying in its correct position on the cabinet, screw the front in place with three 1½-inch, number-eight flathead wood screws (Figs. 6-116 and 6-117).

Before proceeding further, sand the entire clock cabinet and apply some type of finish. The finish can be stain and varnish or any other the

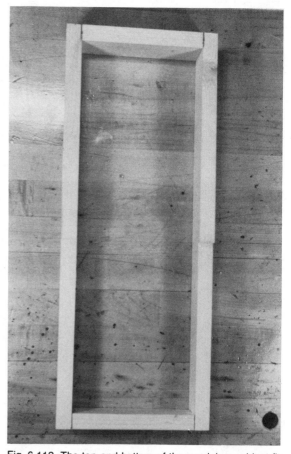

Fig. 6-112. The top and bottom of the pendulum cabinet fit between the two sides.

design is shown in Fig. 6-113. Using a router and any decorative bit, rout the sides and bottom of the pendulum cabinet front and also all eight edges of the octagon.

After sanding the pendulum cabinet and the pendulum cabinet front, glue the front onto the cabinet. The front fits into the ½-inch-×-8¾-inch cutout on the side pendulum cabinet. Place the pendulum cabinet on the back of the octagon clock front. Line up the cabinet to ensure proper location on the octagon (Fig. 6-114). It might be necessary to install the movement in order to correctly line up the cabinet. The cabinet top should be 3⅛ inches from the top edge of the octagon front. When the proper position has been determined, trace the outline of the pendulum cabinet on the rear of the

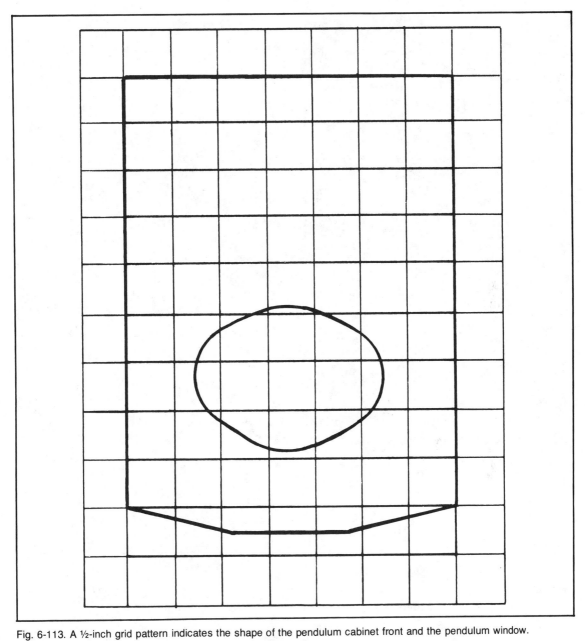

Fig. 6-113. A ½-inch grid pattern indicates the shape of the pendulum cabinet front and the pendulum window.

craftsman selects. Install the movement into the clock cabinet, hang the pendulum, and attach the dial and bezel to the octagon clock front. Allow the clock to run for several hours in this manner to test the component parts of the clock cabinet combined with the clock movement.

After any necessary corrections have been completed, install the ¼-inch-thick, 5¾-inch-×-17⅛-inch clock back. This is held in place by screwing four ½-inch-long, number-six flathead screws through the clock back into the four corner supports.

Fig. 6-114. Lay the pendulum cabinet on the octagon wood front, placing it in the correct position.

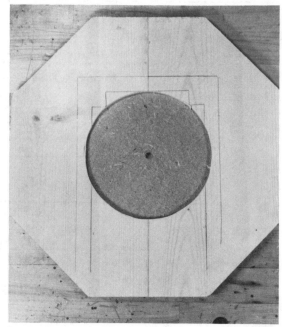

Fig. 6-115. The location of the three screw holes that connect the octagon front to the pendulum cabinet.

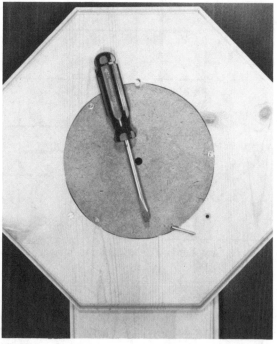

Fig. 6-116. Screw the octagon clock front to the pendulum cabinet.

The octagon schoolhouse clock will always be a favorite of Americans. This clock, which conjures up thoughts of the one-room schoolhouses and patient hand craftsmanship, is sure to be a favorite product of any craftsman's shop.

THE ONTARIO

The Ontario (Fig. 6-118) is an elegant wall clock reminiscent of early weight-driven wall clocks. It is made of a wood clock front, a small wood movement compartment, an attractive brass dial, a pendulum clock movement, and a set of weight shells and chains. The actual wood parts of this attractive clock are relatively few, making it a clock that is quick to build. See Tables 6-14 and 6-15. It is not

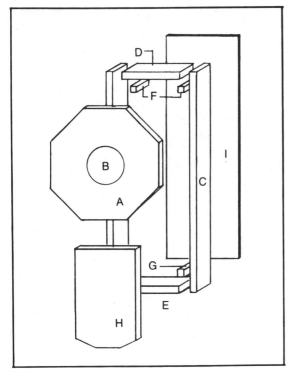

Fig. 6-117. An exploded view showing the wood parts of the schoolhouse-style clock. (The movement, dial, and bezel used in this project have been provided by Klockit.)

6-119 and also in cross-sectional drawing of the turning in Fig. 6-120. This design or almost any other can be turned, but there are a few factors that must be consistent. The wood at the middle of the clock front, the area covered by the dial, should be no more than ½ of an inch thick.

Remove the faceplate from the turned clock front. Draw a 5-inch-diameter circle at the center of the clock front, and cut it out on a jigsaw. Along the 5-inch-diameter edge, rout a ¼-inch-deep and ½-inch-wide rabbet joint around the edge (Fig. 6-121).

Cut a ¼-inch-thick, 6-inch-diameter piece of Masonite or plywood to fit into the rabbeted edge of the center hole. At the center of the 6-inch-diameter disk, drill a ⅜-inch-clock, movement, hand-shaft hole. The disk is screwed into the rabbet

necessarily an expensive clock, but the time involved in building this clock is minimal.

Construction begins by using a large compass or trammel points to draw a 12-inch-diameter circle on part A. This is the clock front, measuring 2 inches thick, 12 inches wide, and 12 inches long. Using a bandsaw, or some other saw capable of cutting curves in thick wood, cut out the circular shape of the clock front. At the center of the circle, drill a small hole; the hole should be no larger than ¼ of an inch in diameter. The hole is drilled to mark the center. Once drilled, it's impossible to lose the center. It cannot be sanded off or accidentally erased.

Mount a lathe faceplate on the back of the 12-inch diameter clock front. Turn the clock front to the desired shape. It is not the intention of this book to teach the proper use of the wood lathe. Therefore, instructions for turning have been omitted.

The example for this section is shown in Fig.

Fig. 6-118. The Ontario clock.

135

Table 6-14. Ontario Clock Materials.

Part	Quantity	Size	Description
A	1	1½″ × 12″ × 12″	wood clock front
B	1	¼″ × 6″ diameter	center clock disk
C	2	¾″ × 1¼″ × 6″	cabinet sides
D	1	¾″ × 1¼″ × 4½″	cabinet top
	2	½″, number six	flathead wood screws
	1	8″ diameter	dial
	1	14″ to 20″ pendulum	clock movement
	1		set of hands to fit
	1		set of weight shells (optional)

of the clock front with two ½-inch long, number-six screws.

The clock movement cabinet is made of three parts: two parts C and one part D. The cabinet sides (parts C) are ¾ of an inch thick, 1¼ inches wide, and 6 inches long. The cabinet top is the same thickness

Fig. 6-119. The design of the wood clock front.

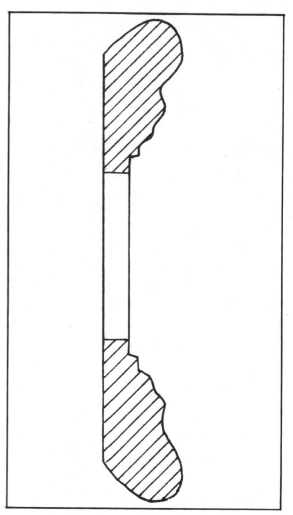

Fig. 6-120. The cross-section view indicates the design of the wood clock front.

and width, but it is 4½ inches long. If this cabinet is not large enough for a particular movement, it can be enlarged. Glue the cabinet between the two sides as shown in Figs. 6-122 and 6-123.

Table 6-15. Erie Clock Materials.

Quantity	Size	Description
1	1½″ × 14″ diameter	wood clock front
1	¼″ × 6″ diameter	mounting board
1	mini	battery movement
1	9½″ diameter	dial
1		set of hands to fit

Fig. 6-121. A rabbet joint is routed around the inside edge of the 5-inch center.

When the movement cabinet assembly has dried, glue it onto the back of the circular wood clock front. All of the wood parts of the Ontario have been cut and assembled. All that remains is to stain and varnish the clock and assemble the clock movement and dial.

The weight shells shown on the sample clock are not functional. They are only for decorative purposes. The shells are hung by chains from two screws that are screwed into the sides of the movement cabinet.

The Ontario is a handsome wall clock very striking in appearance. The deep, dark color of the wood clock front—combined with the brass of the dial and weight shells—creates an eye-catching contrast. The Ontario is sure to be a favorite of the

Fig. 6-122. The cabinet top is glued between the two sides.

craftsman and the admirers of his work. See also Fig. 6-124.

CONNECTICUT WALL CLOCK

The Connecticut wall clock (Fig. 6-125) is another replica of a classic clock of yesteryear. This clock style dates back to the mid-1820s. The Connecticut wall clock was at that time an extremely popular clock on the East Coast of America. The process of building this clock has been changed compared to

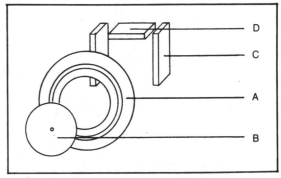

Fig. 6-123. The exploded view of the Ontario clock showing its wood component parts. (The movement, dial, bezel, and hardware used in this example are courtesy of Klockit.)

Fig. 6-124. The Erie clock is an alternate design to the Ontario clock.

Fig. 6-125. Connecticut wall clock.

the original. The changes have been made to simplify construction. The case and door are assembled with butt joints, although the cabinet joints are reinforced with corner blocks. See Table 6-16.

Begin by cutting the two sides (parts A). They will measure ¾ of an inch thick, 3¼ inches wide, and 21 inches long. The two parts B are the next to be cut. These will be the top and bottom. They

should be ½ inch thick, 4½ inches wide, and 11⅜ inches long. Next cut six ¾-inch-×-¾-inch-×-2⅝-inch-long corner supports. Four of the corner blocks will be glued to the sides (parts A). The corner blocks must be held flush with the ends and set in ¼ inch from one edge (Fig. 6-126). There are also two other corner blocks to be glued on the sides. These will be located 9½ inches down from the top end of the sides (Fig. 6-127). These corner blocks are used to support the dial-mounting board.

Cut the back board of the clock. This board can be either ¼-inch-thick Masonite or plywood. The back should be 9¼ inches wide and 21 inches long. As shown in Fig. 6-128, drill a ⅛-inch hole through the back into the four corner blocks. Then use four ½-inch, number-six flathead wood screws to attach the back to the sides.

Table 6-16. Connecticut Wall Clock Materials.

Part	Quantity	Size	Description
A	2	¾″ ×3¼″ × 21″	cabinet sides
B	2	½″ × 4½″ × 11⅜″	cabinet top & bottom
C	6	¾″ × ¾″ × 2″	corner blocks
D	1	¼″ × 9¼″ × 21″	cabinet back
E	1	¼″ × 9½″ × 9¼″	dial mounting board
F	2	½″ × 1½″ × 21″	door rails
G	1	½″ × 1½″ × 7⅞″	top door spreader
H	1	½″ × 1⅞″ × 7⅞″	bottom door spreader
I	1	½″ × ½″ × 7⅞″	middle door spreader
J	2	½″ × 1½″ × 1½″	top door trim
K	2	½″ × 1½″ × 1⅞″	bottom door trim
	4	½″, number six	flathead wood screws
	4	½″, number six	roundhead wood screws
	8	¾″, number eight	flathead wood screws
	1	7⅞″ square	dial
	1	12 to 14 inch	pendulum movement
	1		set of hands to fit
	1	⅛″ × 8⅜″ × 9⅞″	window glass

Fig. 6-126. Corner blocks are glued to the ends of the sides. They must be held flush with the ends and set ¼ of an inch from the edges.

Part E, the dial-mounting board, is made of ¼-inch-thick Masonite or plywood. The board is 9¼ inches wide and 9½ inches long. At the four corners of the mounting board are ⅛-inch holes drilled through. These holes are located ⅜ of an inch in from the sides and ⅜ of an inch in from the top and bottom. The clock-movement, hand-shaft hole is 4⅝ inches in from the side and 4¼ inches up from the bottom. At this position, drill the ⅜-inch, hand-shaft hole (Fig. 6-129).

With four-inch, number-six roundhead screws, secure the clock front to the ends of the corner blocks through the four ½-inch holes previously drilled (Fig. 6-130). The top and bottom (parts B) are the next to be screwed to the clock cabinet

assembly. Drill four 3/16-inch holes in both the top and bottom. The positions of the holes are shown in Fig. 6-131. On the top side of parts B, the 3/16-inch holes are counterbored with a ⅜-inch drill bit. Once the ¾-inch, number-eight screws are tightened into the sides—securing the top and bottom to the cabinet—the ⅜-inch holes are filled with either furniture buttons or dowel rod.

The clock cabinet door is next to be built. The door consists of two side rails and three spreaders. The rails (parts F) are ½ of inch thick, 1½ inches wide, and 21 inches long. The top spreader is ½ of an inch thick (as are all door parts), 1½ inches wide, and 7⅞ inches long. The bottom spreader (part H) is 1⅞ inches wide by 7⅞ inches long. The middle spreader is the same thickness and length, but ½ of an inch wide.

Fig. 6-127. Two additional corner blocks are glued onto the sides, 9½ inches down from the top end.

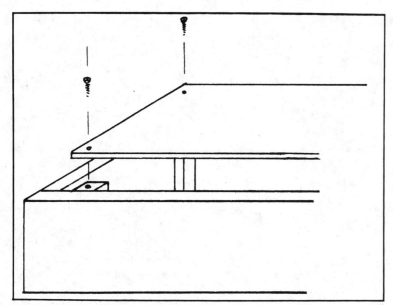

Fig. 6-128. Drill a ⅛-inch-diameter hole through the clock cabinet back into the center of the corner blocks.

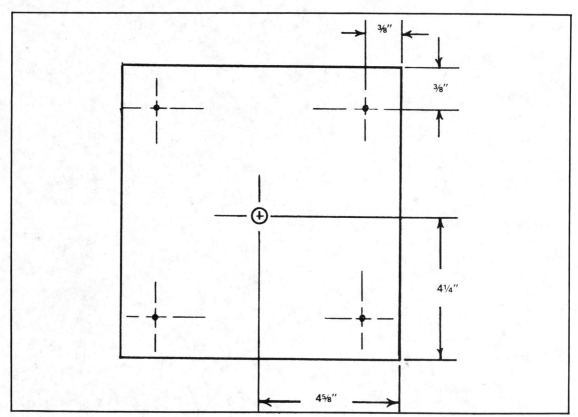

Fig. 6-129. The dial mounting board requires five holes to be drilled through it. The location of these holes is found in the drawing.

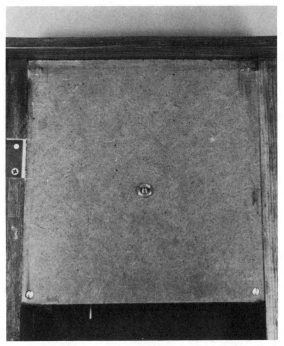

Fig. 6-130. Screw the dial mounting board to the corner blocks.

Glue the door parts together with the top and bottom spreader even with the ends of the rails and the top edge of the middle spreader 7⅞ inches down from the bottom of the top spreader (Figs. 6-132 and 6-133).

The inside edge of the lower window of the door receives a 3/16-inch deep,¼-inch-wide edge rabbet. The rabbet is cut so that a ⅛-inch-thick, 8⅜-inch-×-9⅞-inch pane of glass can be inserted. The upper window of the door does not have glass.

On the front of the door there are four decorative trim boards located on the top and bottom of the door rails. The top door trim parts measure ½ of an inch thick, 1½ inches wide, and 1½ inches long. The bottom door trim pieces are also ½ of an inch thick and 1½ inches wide, but 1⅞ inches long. Glue these into position on the door. The project photographed in this section has two 17¾-inch-long decorative moldings. These two trim boards are optional, and they need not be incorporated into the clock cabinet.

After staining and varnishing all wood parts and painting the Masonic back flat black, the clock is

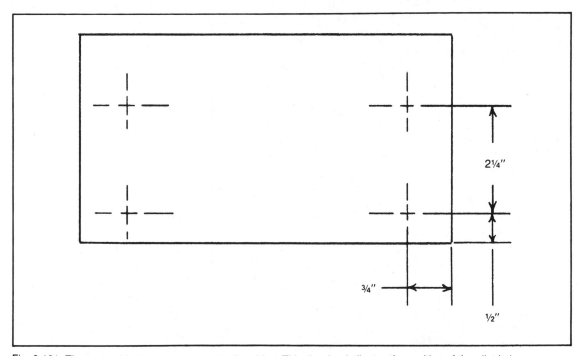

Fig. 6-131. The top and bottom are screwed to the sides. This drawing indicates the position of the pilot holes.

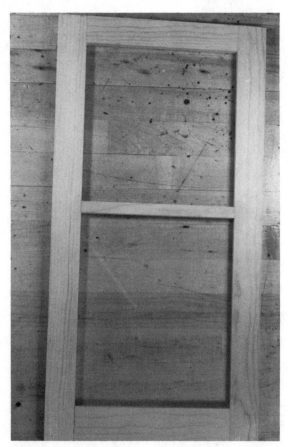

Fig. 6-132. The door to the Connecticut wall clock is made up of two side rails, top and bottom spreaders, and a middle spreader.

ready for final assembly. Two hinges need to be screwed onto the left side of the door and a door catch should be used to hold the door closed. The clock movement and 7⅞-inch-square dial are both attached to the dial mounting board. Follow the hanging directions that accompany the clock movement being used to determine how it is best attached to the mounting board.

The Connecticut wall clock, with its straight simple lines, is a relatively easy clock to build because it does not have any curved or irregular shapes. Also, other than the routing of the edge rabbet on the door, the clock cabinet does not require a large investment in woodworking machines. The resulting clock cabinet is a splendid example of the type of clock found in early American homes.

SHAKER-STYLE WALL CLOCK

The Shaker Style wall clock (Fig. 6-134) is an adaptation of those found in early Shaker households. Its unusual appearance is a result of a combination of simplistic construction and functionality. By virtue of its large size and clean, straight lines, it makes an impressive addition to any room in the house.

This clock has been designed with the ease of construction in mind, although it is a large clock with many parts. By following the step-by-step instructions, it is relatively easy to build.

Begin the construction by cutting to size the four basic components of the cabinet, the two sides, top, and bottom pieces. See Table 6-17. The sides, parts A and B, are ¾ of an inch thick, 4¼ inches wide, and 41 inches long. The top and bottom, parts C and D, are 3 inches thick, 6 inches wide, and 15

Table 6-17. Shaker-Style Wall Clock Materials.

Part	Quantity	Size	Description
A	1	¾″ × 4¼″ × 41″	side
B	1	¾″ × 4¼″ × 41″	side
C	1	¾″ × 6″ × 15½″	top
D	1	¾″ × 6″ × 15½″	bottom
E	4	¾″ × ¾″ × 3¾″	corner braces
F	4	¾″ × ¾″ × 3¼″	dial supports
G	4	¾″ × 2″ × 10″	horizontal door parts
H	2	¾″ × 2″ × 14″	vertical door parts
I	2	¾″ × 2″ × 26″	bottom vertical door parts
J	1	¾″ × 12″ × 12½″	dial frame
K	1	¾″ × 1½″ × 14″	door divider
L	1	¼″ × 10¾″ × 12″	dial mounting board (plywood)
M	1	⅛″ × 12½″ × 41″	back (plywood or Masonite)
	8	¾″, number 8	roundhead screws
	4	1½″, number 6	flathead screws
	1	9½″ diameter	round dial (metal, ceramic, or paper)
	1	26 to 29″ pendulum	movement (battery, windup, or weight driven)
	1	sized to fit	set of hands
	1		set of weight shells, decorative or functional
	1	⅛″ × 10⅝″ × 10⅝″	upper door glass unit
	1	⅛″ × 10⅝″ × 22¾″	lower door glass unit
	4		decorative or butt hinges
	2		magnetic catches
	2		pull knobs

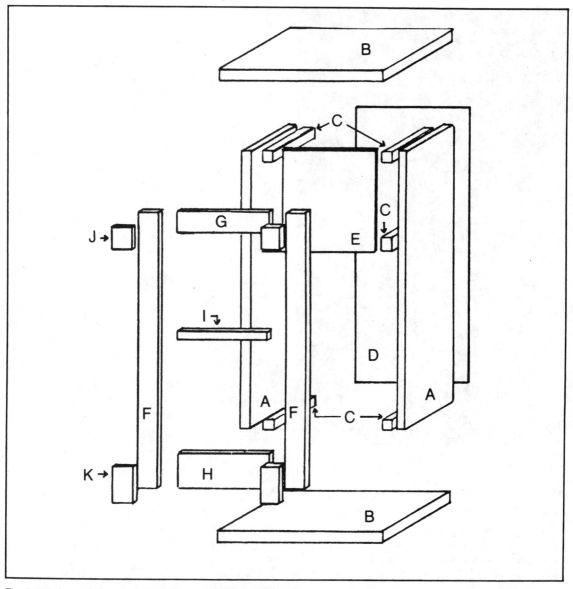

Fig. 6-133. An exploded view of the Connecticut wall clock showing its wood parts. (The movement, dial, and hardware are courtesy of Klockit.)

inches long. Also cut the six corner braces (F) to their ¾-inch-×-¾-inch-×-3¾-inch size.

On the top and bottom (parts C and D), draw two lines 1½ inches in from both ends. Also on these pieces draw a line ¼ inch in from the back edge. Glue two of the corner blocks to the top and two to the bottom. These should be 1½ inches in

from the sides along the lines. The end should be on the ¼-inch line (Fig. 6-135).

After time to dry, use a file and sandpaper—or a router with a ½-inch beading bit—to round the two ends and front edge of parts C and D. If a router is used, the routing must be done before the corner blocks are glued on.

Fig. 6-134. Shaker-style wall clock.

doors have dried, rout a ¼-inch-deep, ½-inch-wide rabbet on the inside edge to hold the glass (Fig. 6-137).

The clock cabinet assembly will need four ¾-×-¾-×-1¼-inch dial supports (F). These will be located ¾ of an inch in from the front edge. The top support is 2¾ inches from the top, while the lower support is 12 inches from the top. Glue the supports into position (Fig. 6-138).

This clock has a ¼-inch-thick plywood dial mounting board (K) as do many clocks, but it also has a dial frame (J). The dial frame is ¾ of an inch thick, 12 inches wide, and 12½ inches long.

Draw a light pencil line on the dial frame from the upper right to the lower left corner. Then draw another from the upper left to the lower right

Fig. 6-135. Glue two corner blocks to the top and bottom parts, C and D. These must be 1½ inches from the ends.

Sand the surfaces of A, B, C, and D. It is easier to sand them while they are separate than when they are assembled.

To fasten the sides to the top and bottom, glue the corner braces on the sides. The back edge of the sides must be kept even with the back edge of parts C and D (Fig. 6-136).

While the clock cabinet assembly is drying, cut the wood for the two cabinet doors. You will need four ¾-×-2-×-10-inch (G), two ¾-×-2-×-14-inch (H), and two ¾-×-2-×-26-inch (I) pieces. Lightly sand all of these parts before their assembly.

Glue parts G between parts H. Allow ample time for this door unit to dry before it is moved. Follow these same instructions for assembling the bottom door unit (parts G and I). When the two

Fig. 6-136. Glue the sides to the corner blocks of the top and bottom. The back edge of the sides must be kept flush with the back edge of the top and bottom.

screws to hold the dial frame in place. Make sure the screw heads are slightly recessed below the surface so that they won't interfere with the door. Do not glue the dial frame on. There might be an occasion to remove it in the future to repair or replace the dial or movement.

Obtain a piece of ¼-inch-thick plywood or Masonite. This will be 10¾-×-12-inch, dial-mounting board (part L). The mounting board will not be visible when the clock is completed; therefore it is not necessary that this be new material.

As with the dial frame, find the center of the mounting board by drawing the two diagonal lines from corner to corner. Where these two lines cross, drill the hand-shaft hole. This is usually ⅜ of an inch, but check the movement.

Fig. 6-137. The two doors require a rabbet joint on the inside rear edge to accept the door glass.

corner. Where these two lines cross is the center of the board. At this point, draw a 9½-inch-diameter circle. Carefully cut out this circle and sand the inside edge of it. The front edge of the circle can be rounded with a file, router, or left as it is (Fig. 6-139).

To mount the dial frame to the clock cabinet, drill four 3/16-inch holes. The two at the top should be ⅜ of an inch from the outside edge and 2 5/16 inches down from the top edge. The two lower holes will be located ⅜ of an inch from each side, and ½ of an inch up from the bottom (Fig. 6-139). These holes should line up with the ends of the dial supports. Sand the dial frame before attaching it to the cabinet. Use four 1½-inch, number-six flathead

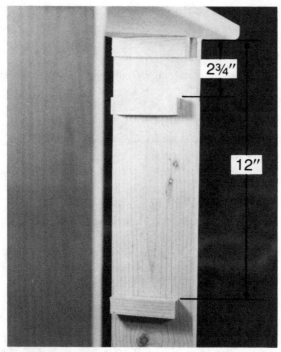

Fig. 6-138. Glue four dial supports (parts F) onto the inside of the sides.

Fig. 6-140. Install the mounting board to the clock movement.

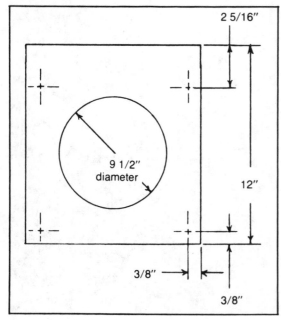

Fig. 6-139. The dial frame requires a 9½-inch-diameter hole to be cut out of the center, and four mounting screw holes.

The method to attach the dial to the board varies as to what type of dial is being used. Some metal dials have small holes drilled through them where tiny screws or brads hold it to the mounting board.

If a paper or cardboard dial is to be used, the best way to mount it is to use rubber cement. This is the contact cement that is found in the school supply section of most stores. Apply a thin layer of cement to the back of the dial in a place where it will not show in order to check if the cement damages the paper. If there is no problem with the test spot, apply a thin layer to the back of the dial and also a layer to the mounting board. When both of these are dry, carefully line up the hand-shaft holes on both dial and mounting board; make sure the 12 is centered at the top. Once these two have been placed together, it is virtually impossible to separate them without damaging the paper dial.

If a metal, ceramic, or heavy cardboard dial is to be used, it can be fastened to the mounting board by using the hand shaft, washer, and mounting nut that come with the movement.

Drill four 3/16-inch screw pilot holes in the mounting board. These should be located so as to go through the mounting board without coming too close to the dial. Install the mounting board by screwing four ¾-inch, number-eight roundhead screws through the 3/16-diameter holes into the dial frame. The dial must be centered in the 9½-diameter hole cut in the dial frame (Fig. 6-140).

The movement can be put in place at this time, providing it has not been installed previously to hold on the dial. Follow the directions with the movement as to the mounting procedure.

Cut the back out of a sheet of ¼-inch-thick plywood or Masonite. The size is 12½ inches wide and 41 inches long. Check to see if it will fit in the cabinet. The back should fit between the sides up against the end of the corner blocks. Drill four 3/16-inch screw pilot holes through the back so it can be screwed into the ends of the corner blocks. These holes should be located ⅜ of an inch in from the ends of the back panel. Fasten it with four ¾-inch, number-eight roundhead screws.

By this time, the two door units have had plenty of time to dry. To give them a professional appearance, slightly round the outside edges of both doors. This can be done with a router if one is available. It is best to sand and apply stain or var-

Fig. 6-142. The door divider (part K) is glued to the sides, between the top and bottom doors.

Fig. 6-141. Example of a butt hinge and butterfly hinge.

nish to the doors before screwing on the hinges. Otherwise, applying the finish to the cabinet will be difficult with the doors in the way. It is also a good time to apply the finish to the entire clock cabinet as well as to the doors.

There are basically two types of hinges that can be used to hold the doors to the cabinet. These are common butt hinges and the decorative hinges (Fig. 6-141).

The butt hinge is a stronger hinge because it is recessed into the wood of the cabinet. This is a time-consuming operation that requires accurate work with a hammer and chisel. With the butt hinge, the only part of the hinge that will be exposed is the pivoting barrel.

The decorative hinge does not have the strength of the butt hinge, although it should be strong enough to support the weight of the clock doors. It does not require the removal of wood as does the butt hinge. It is mounted with screws directly onto the surface of the wood. These hinges are much easier to install and have a pleasing appearance, although the butt hinge is much stronger. The choice of hinges is up to the craftsman.

When fastening the doors to the clock cabinet, hold the top door slightly away from the top of the cabinet. This opening should be no more than 1/16 of an inch. The same thing applies to the lower door and the bottom. When the doors are on in this manner, there should be a ⅞-inch gap between them. This area is filled with a ¾-inch thick, 1½-inch wide, 14-inch-long door divider (part K). The divider has the ends and two edges slightly rounded (Figs. 6-142 and 6-143).

Glue the door divider onto the cabinet sides.

Center it between the two closed doors. There should be a 1/16-inch clearance between the doors and the divider.

The Shaker-style clock, with its large cabinet, will look rather bare with only a pendulum gracefully swinging in the pendulum window. To alter this situation, a weight-driven movement that requires weight shells and chains hanging in the pendulum compartment can be used. The same appearance can be obtained by using a less expensive movement and hanging a set of nonfunctional weight shells. These can be hung from small screws or eye hooks screwed into the back of the dial frame or mounting board.

The weight shells are an option that the craftsman might prefer to choose for his clock. Some other options that can be used to individualize

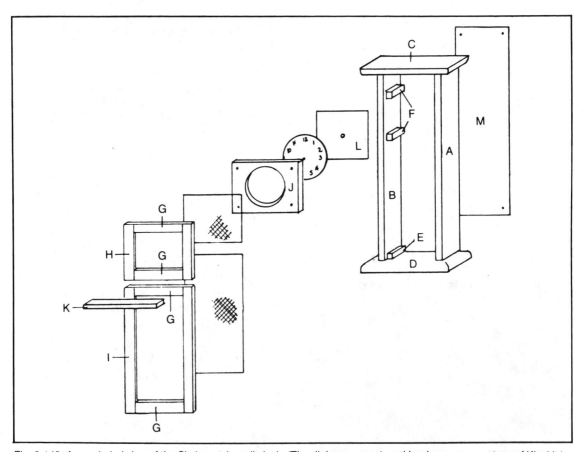

Fig. 6-143. An exploded view of the Shaker-style wall clock. (The dial, movement, and hardware are courtesy of Klockit.)

the Shaker-style clock is the choice of pull knobs used on the two doors. These can be of almost any variety. Also the interior of the pendulum compartment can be painted a dark color. This should provide a background that will highlight the pendulum and weight shells.

The Shaker-style wall clock, with its large cabinet and classic shaker style, will quickly become an heirloom within the family. It also makes a great wedding gift that is sure to become a treasured memory.

THE HURON

The Huron (Fig. 6-144) is an elegant clock that is reminiscent of the clock cabinets often used with the famous regulator clock movements. They came in several sizes. The large versions were as tall as 6

Table 6-18. Huron Clock Materials.

Part	Quantity	Size	Description
A	2	1/2″ × 2″ × 23 1/4″	front side rails
B	1	1/2″ × 4 1/4″ × 5 3/4″	front top
C	1	1/2″ × 2″ × 5 3/4″	front bottom
D	4	1/2″ × 1 1/2″ × 23 1/4″	side rails
E	2	1/2″ × 2″ × 8 3/4″	side tops
F	2	1/2″ × 2″ × 2″	side bottoms
G	4	3/4″ × 3/4″ × 4 3/4″	corner supports
H	1	1/4″ × 8 3/4″ × 23 1/4″	back
I	1	3/4″ × 5 7/8″ × 10 7/16″	first top decorative trim
J	1	3/4″ × 6 5/16″ × 11 3/16″	second top decorative trim
K	1	3/4″ × 5 5/8″ × 9 5/8″	first bottom decorative trim
L	1	3/4″ × 5″ × 8 3/4″	second bottom decorative trim
M	1	3/4″ × 4 5/8″ × 8″	third bottom decorative trim
	4	1 1/4″, number six	roundhead wood screws
	1	1/8″ × 6 3/8″ × 19 5/8″	front glass
	2	1/8″ × 2 5/8″ × 13 1/2″	side glass

Fig. 6-144. The Huron clock.

or 7 feet, and frequently appeared in jewelry stores and banks. The home model, as discussed in this section, is much smaller than those used for commercial purposes, but uses the same type of regulator movement.

Construction begins by cutting out the side rails for the clock front (parts A). See Table 6-18. These measure ½ of an inch, 2 inches wide, and 23¼ inches long. The top of the front is—as all front and side parts— ½ of an inch thick, 4¼ inches wide, and 5¾ inches long. The grain onparts B and C, the front top and bottom, run horizontally. When finished, the grain running up and down the sides, and side to side on the top and bottom, provide a handsome contrast.

On part B, the front top, there is a 2⅞-inch radius arc cut out of the bottom (Fig. 6-145). On the back side of part A, once the arc has been cut, there will be a recess cut out. The recess will be used later to hold the glass which is inserted in the front and sides (Fig. 6-146). The recess is 3/16 of an inch deep, 2¼ inches wide, and extends across the length of the part. Glue the four front pieces together into the front door (Fig. 6-147).

The two sides are made up of parts D, E, and F, and are constructed in the same manner as the front. All that differs is the size of the parts. Parts D are 23¼ inches long and 1 ½ inches wide. Parts E,

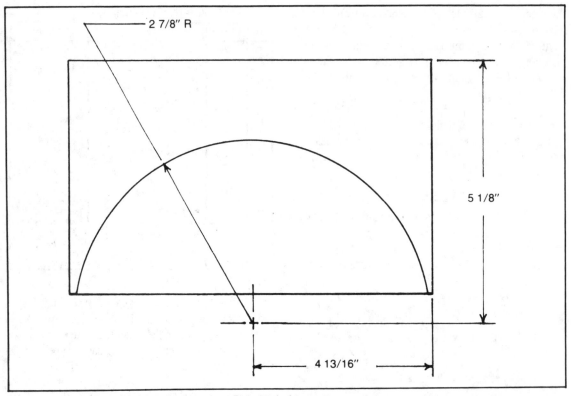

2 7/8" R

5 1/8"

4 13/16"

Fig. 6-145. The radius of the door front top (part B) is 2⅞ inches.

the side tops, are 2 inches wide by 2 inches long. The arc cutout of Part E has a recess cut out as in the rear of the front top (Fig. 6-148). When the recess has been cut and all parts are ready, glue the parts together to form the left and right sides.

The inside of the door and sides require that an edge rabbet be cut along the inside edge (Fig. 6-149). This rabbet is cut to receive the glass. The rabbet is cut with a ½-inch rabbeting bit in a router. The depth of the cut is 3/16 of an inch; that is the same as the depth of the recess previously cut in the top parts.

On the top and bottom of the side panels, glue a ¾-×-¾-×-4¾-inch-long corner block (Fig. 6-150). These blocks are glued flush with the ends of the sides and flush with the front edge. The rear of the block is set in ¼ of an inch from the rear edge of the side panels.

Next, cut the back of the clock cabinet (part H). The back can be made of the same wood as the rest

Fig. 6-146. The 3/16-inch-deep-by-2¼-inch wide recess is for glass that will later be inserted.

Fig. 6-147. Clamp the door together keeping the surfaces flat.

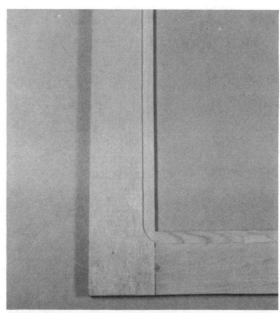

Fig. 6-149. Cut a 3/16-inch-deep-by-½-inch-wide edge rabbet joint along the inside edge of the door. This will hold the glass.

Fig. 6-148. The cabinet sides require a 3/16-inch deep and a ⅞-inch wide recess.

Fig. 6-150. Corner blocks are glued flush with the ends of the two sides. The blocks must be kept ¼ inch from the rear edge of the sides.

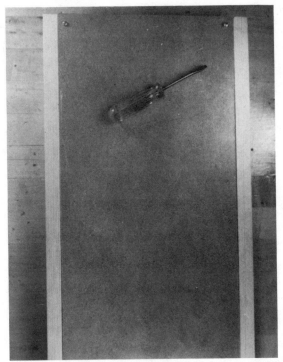

Fig. 6-151. The back is held to the clock cabinet by screwing through the back into the corner blocks.

of the clock, ¼-inch-thick plywood, or ¼-inch-thick Masonite painted black (as in the example). The back size is 8¾ inches wide and 23¾ inches long. Drill four ⅛-inch holes through the back at the location of the corner blocks. With four 1¼-inch, number-six roundhead screws, attach the back to the sides (Fig. 6-151).

Lay the front door on the sides and back assembly. Make sure the door and sides fit together properly. If any work is required to assure a good fit, it should be done now. Apply the hinges to the left side of the cabinet and attach the front door to the rest of the cabinet.

The next operation is to cut the decorative trim pieces found on the cabinet top and bottom. These parts are cut to size and then routed with either an ogee router bit or a cove router bit (Fig. 6-152).

Rout the first top decorative trim board with the ogee bit. Rout one edge and the two sides. The rear edge is to remain square. Part J, the second top decorative trim board, is routed with the cove bit. Again, only rout the front edge and two sides.

The three bottom trim boards are made by

Fig. 6-152. Examples of results of the ogee (left) and cove (right) router bits.

Fig. 6-153. Glue the top and bottom trim boards together.

following the procedure as for those of the top. The first board (part K) and the third (part M), are routed with the cove router bit. The second trim board (part L) is routed with the ogee bit.

Glue the two top trim boards together (parts I and J). Make sure the routed edge of part J lines up with the top edge of part I (Fig. 6-153). Also glue the three parts of the bottom trim boards together as previously done with those of the top.

Sand all parts, including the routed edges, if they have not been sanded thus far. It is advisable that the clock cabinet be stained at this time before the top and bottom trim boards are glued to the cabinet.

Once the stain has had an opportunity to dry, glue the top and bottom to the cabinet assembly. *Note:* Glue to the sides and corner blocks, not to the front door. The door must open (Fig. 6-154).

Install the movement and dial in the clock cabinet. The following instructions provide two methods that can be used. Both of these methods

Fig. 6-154. The top and bottom trim board assemblies are glued to the top and bottom of the sides.

Fig. 6-155. The Klockit movement used in this sample has a mounting bracket built into the movement.

will need to be adapted to fit the particular movement being used.

The movement used in the sample clock is a combination windup movement and dial. On the back of the movement there is a mounting bracket that supports the movement from the back (Figs. 6-155 and 156). This type of mounting procedure is by far the easiest method, but not all clock movements are so equipped. An alternate method might be necessary to hang the movement from the top. A ¼-inch-thick piece of plywood is glued and screwed to a ¾-×-¾-inch support block that is glued and screwed to the top (part I). Through the ¼-inch plywood, drill a ⅜-inch hole for the movement hand-shaft to extend through. The dial will be held in place on the outside of the plywood by the hand-shaft nut.

These alternate movement hanging instruc-

tions are vague, with no dimensions given, but it is vague for a reason. There are many styles of movements that each require its own individual treatment to be hung.

Remove the dial and movement from the cabinet. The entire cabinet is varnished with a finish of the craftsman's choice. On the sample built as shown in the illustrations, the Masonite back has been painted flat black. If using plywood or solid lumber, the same stain that is on the cabinet could be used.

After final assembling of the movement and dial in the cabinet, install the three glass panes. The size of the glass panes is listed in Table 6-18. The glass panes can be held in the edge rabbet joints in a number of ways. Push points are the most obvious, but they cannot always be used in all instances—especially with hard woods. Also, clear cellophane

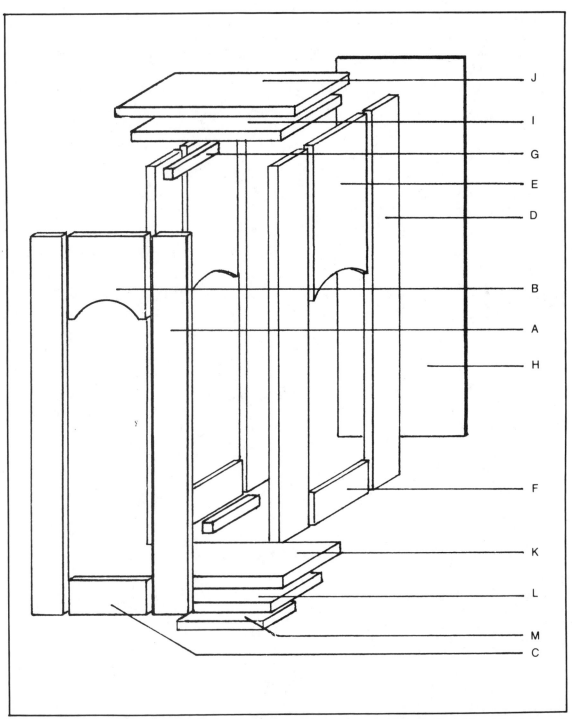

Fig. 6-156. An exploded view of the Huron showing the wood parts necessary to build it as described. (The windup movement used in this example has been supplied courtesy of Klockit Company.)

packaging tape can be used to safely hold the glass in place.

The Huron is an impressive clock cabinet reminiscent of the best of the past. The following, glazed sides and front and the beautiful dial and pendulum lend to its distinctive appearance.

Chapter 7

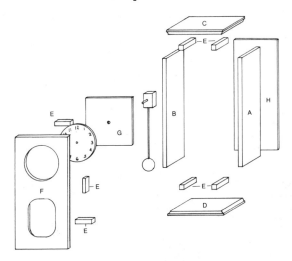

Quickie Clocks

MOST OF THE CLOCKS THUS FAR DESCRIBED in this book have been heavily dependent on woodworking. The following clocks take advantage of the modern battery movements that only require a ⅜-inch-diameter hole to be drilled for the movement hand-shaft to fit through.

The clocks in this chapter cover a broad scope of ideas. These are by no means the only clocks that can be built. Quickie clocks are limited only by the imagination of the craftsman. There are many sources for quickie clocks. Just about anything can be used. Watch antique stores, garage sales, flea markets, or any other store for materials that might be turned into clocks.

FLOOR-TILE CLOCK

Materials

One 12-inch square self-adhesive floor tile.

One ¼-inch-thick mounting board the same size as the tile.

One battery movement.

One set of hands to fit.

One set of hour markers.

Instructions

1. Cut the backboard the same size as the tile.

2. Glue the tile to the board.

3. Drill a ⅜-inch hole through the center.

4. Insert the battery movement. A miniquartz movement will permit the clock to hang closer to the wall.

5. Apply the hour markers.

6. Hang by the clock movement hanging bracket (Fig. 7-1).

DISC AND DIAL CLOCK

Materials

One 12-inch-diameter wood disc.

One 7-to-9-inch-diameter dial.

One battery movement.

One set of hands to fit.

Fig. 7-2. A circular wooden disc and a commercial dial combine to produce this attractive clock.

Fig. 7-1. A self-adhesive floor tile can quickly be made into a beautiful clock with very little work.

Instructions

    1. Cut a 12-inch-diameter disc.

    2. In the center of the disc, cut out a hole large enough for the movement.

    3. Sand, stain, and varnish the disc.

    4. Glue the dial to the disc.

    5. Install the battery movement.

    6. Hang the clock by the hanging bracket on the clock movement (Fig. 7-2).

QUARRY-TILE CLOCK

Materials

    One ceramic tile (any size).

    One battery movement.

    One set of hands to fit.

    One set of hour markers.

Instructions

    1. Locate the center of the ceramic tile.

    2. Drill a ⅜-inch hole through the tile with a masonry bit.

    3. Install the clock movement.

Fig. 7-3. A ceramic quarry tile can be used to create an unusual clock.

Fig. 7-4. Almost any framed picture can also become a clock, with the addition of a minibattery movement.

4. Locate and apply the hour markers.

5. Hang the clock with the hanger bracket on the movement.

6. A wood frame could be built to surround the tile (Fig. 7-3).

PICTURE CLOCK

Materials

> One print in a frame—no glass.
> One miniquartz battery movement.
> One set of hands to fit.
> One set of hour markers.

Instructions

1. Select a print that has at least ½ inch between the wall and the back of the print. (The clock movement needs this room.)

2. Drill a ⅜-inch hole through the print at the location of the clock.

3. Install the movement.

4. Apply the hour markers.

5. Hang the picture as usual (Fig. 7-4).

JELLO-MOLD CLOCK

Materials

> One copper-colored Jello mold.
> One short-shaft battery movement.
> One set of hands to fit.
> One set of hour markers.

Instructions

1. Locate the center of the mold.

2. Drill a ⅜-inch hole through the center.

3. Install the movement.

4. Apply the hour markers.

5. Hang by the ring attached to the mold or by the hanger bracket on the clock movement (Fig. 7-5).

Fig. 7-5. Many kitchens have copper-colored jello molds hanging on their walls. Why not add a clock movement to make a striking wall clock?

Fig. 7-6. The toilet-seat clock might not be found hanging above the fireplace of many homes, but it is a great conversation piece for a recreation room.

TOILET-SEAT CLOCK

Materials

    One toilet seat (wood or plastic).
    One battery movement.
    One set of hands to fit.
    One set of hour markers.

Instructions

    1. Locate the center of the toilet-seat top.
    2. Drill a ⅜-inch hole through the center.
    3. Locate the hour marker locations and apply the markers.
    4. Hang the clock on a strong screw or nail (Fig. 7-6).

PLATE CLOCK

Materials

    One ceramic or plastic plate.
    One ½-inch, hand-shaft movement.
    One set of hands to fit.
    One set of hour markers.

Fig. 7-7. There are many beautiful plates that can be transformed into a functional, attractive clock.

Instructions

1. Find the center of the plate.

2. Drill a ⅜-inch hole through the center. For ceramic plates, use a masonry drill bit.

3. Apply the hour markers—any style.

4. Hang the plate clock by the hanger bracket on the clock movement or with a spring plate hanger (Fig. 7-7).

TENNIS/HANDBALL RACKET CLOCK

Materials

One tennis/handball racket.
One 5-to-6 inch dial.
One battery movement.
One set of hands to fit.

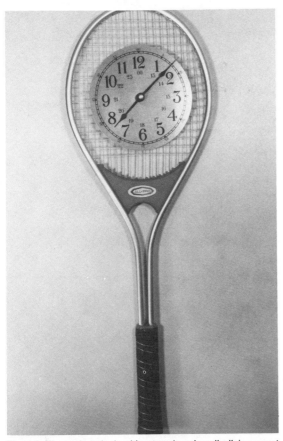

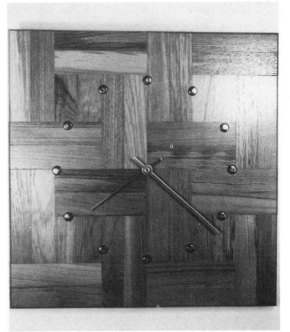

Fig. 7-9. Floor covering stores sell a large selection of wood-floor tiles. These prefinished tiles are assembled into various designs.

Instructions

1. Locate the center of the racket.

2. Insert the battery movement hand-shaft through the weaving, from the back side.

3. On the front, lay the dial and secure it in place with the hand-shaft washer and nut.

4. Hang the racket by any method available (Fig. 7-8).

WOODEN-FLOOR TILE CLOCK

Materials

One wooden-floor tile, 12″ by 12″.
One miniquartz battery movement.
One set of hands to fit.
One set of hour markers.

Instructions

1. Locate the center.

2. Drill a ⅜-inch hole through the center.

3. Insert the movement. A miniquartz movement will permit the tile to hang close to the wall.

4. Apply the hour markers.

Fig. 7-8. The racket clock, either tennis or handball, is a great gift for sports-minded people. It doesn't even require a hole to be drilled.

5. Hang the clock by the hanger bracket on the movement (Fig. 7-9).

EMBROIDERY CLOCK

Materials

One piece of embroidery cloth.

One embroidery hoop, several colors of embroidery thread.

One battery movement.

One set of hands to fit.

Instructions

1. Place the cloth tightly in the hoop.

2. Locate the center.

3. Cut a small hole through the center.

4. Embroider a picture or part of one on the cloth—embroider the hour markers.

5. Install the movement. A piece of cardboard might need to be installed behind the cloth to lend it support).

Fig. 7-11. Any type of hubcap can be used to create an unusual clock for the den, kids' room, or garage.

6. Hang by use of the hanger bracket on the movement (Fig. 7-10).

HUBCAP CLOCK

Materials

One clean, shiny automobile hubcap.

One short-shaft clock movement.

One set of hands (length to fit).

One set of hour markers.

Instructions

1. Find the center of the hubcap (wheel cover).

2. Drill a ⅜-inch hole through the center of the hubcap.

3. Insert the clock movement.

4. Install the clock hands.

5. Apply the hour markers (Fig. 7-11).

FIREPLACE BELLOWS CLOCK

Materials

One fireplace bellows, any size.

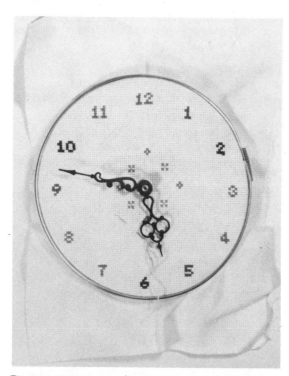

Fig. 7-10. Craft stores sell embroidery clock kits. This clock differs from those in that the embroidery hoop is left on to provide a frame for the clock.

162

One clock movement.
One set of hands to fit.
One set of hour markers.

Instructions

1. Locate the center of the bellows wood front.

2. Drill a ⅜-inch hole through one side.

3. Remove the leather part from the bellows front.

4. Install the battery movement.

5. Replace the leather.

6. Apply some style of hour markers.

7. Hang by a leather strap or another method (Fig. 7-12).

CORK-TILE CLOCK

Materials

Three 12-×-12-inch tiles.

Fig. 7-13. Square cork tiles can be purchased in many stores. The tiles are soft enough to be worked with a knife; thus, no other tools are required.

One battery movement.
One set of hands to fit.
One set of hour markers.

Instructions

1. Locate the center of the cork tiles.

2. Drill a ⅜-inch hole through all three cork tiles.

3. Cut out a 3-×-3-inch square around the ⅜-inch hole on *two* of the tiles. This will form the clock movement cavity.

4. Glue the three cork tiles together with paneling glue or contact cement.

5. Install the movement.

6. Apply the hour markers—anything will work.

7. Hang the clock by the movement hanger (Fig. 7-13).

DRIFTWOOD CLOCK

Materials

One piece of driftwood, any size.

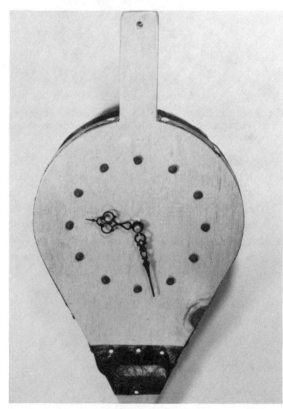

Fig. 7-12. A bellows can often be found hanging next to the fireplace—usually as a decoration. Why not turn it into a functional clock?

One battery movement.
One set of hands to fit.
One set of hour markers.

Instructions

    1. Locate a section of the driftwood where the thickness does not exceed ¾ of an inch.

    2. At this point, drill a ⅜-inch hole.

    3. Install the clock movement.

    4. Apply the hour markers.

    5. Hang on the wall (Fig. 7-14).

BARN-WOOD CLOCK

Materials

    One piece of barn wood, any size.
    One battery movement with long hand-shaft.
    One set of hands to fit.
    One set of hour markers.

Fig. 7-15. Characteristic of barn wood are the attractive, deep, weathered-grain patterns. Add a clock movement and a handsome, rustic clock is the result.

Instructions

    1. Find the location of the hand-shaft hole.

    2. At this location, drill a ⅜-inch hole.

    3. Insert a long-shaft clock movement.

    4. Apply the hour markers. Old nails might be suitable for this clock.

    5. Hang by the clock movement hanger bracket or by conventional hangers (Fig. 7-15).

COOKIE-TIN CLOCK

Materials

    One cookie tin, any size.
    One battery movement.
    One set of hands to fit.
    One set of hour markers.

Instructions

    1. Find the center of the top of the tin.

Fig. 7-14. Driftwood, with its wave-washed gray wood, is a favorite of most decorators. Add a clock movement and produce a beautiful clock.

Fig. 7-16. Many cookie tins have prints of beautiful paintings on their lids. These can be turned into distinctive clocks.

2. Drill a ⅜-inch hole through the top.

3. Install the movement. Replace top on bottom.

4. Apply the hour markers.

5. Hang on the wall by the conventional hanging brackets (Fig. 7-16).

ANTIQUE WOODEN HATBOX CLOCK

Materials

One wooden hatbox.
One battery movement.
One set of hands to fit.
One set of hour markers.

Instructions

1. Locate the center of the hatbox lid.
2. Drill a ⅜-inch hole through the lid.
3. Install the movement.
4. Apply hour markers.

Fig. 7-17. Replicas of antique wood hatboxes are sold in many craft stores. These boxes can be turned into beautiful desk clocks.

5. Hang on the wall or place on a desk or table (Fig. 7-17).

FOOTBALL HELMET DESK CLOCK

Materials

One football helmet.
One battery movement.
One set of hands to fit.
One set of hour markers.

Instructions

1. Locate the position of the hand-shaft hole.
2. Drill a ⅜-inch, hand-shaft hole.
3. Insert the movement.
4. Attach the clock hands.
5. Apply the hour markers.
6. This clock is designed to be placed on a desk or fireplace mantel (Fig. 7-18).

FOOTBALL HELMET WALL CLOCK

Materials

One football helmet.
One large picture frame.
One ¼-inch piece of plywood.
One battery movement.

Fig. 7-19. This clock is created with half of a football helmet, a mounting board, frame, and movement. The other half could be a matching plaque or another clock.

Fig. 7-18. A discarded football helmet requires only a hand-shaft hole, movement, and hour markers to create a great clock for a sports fan.

Fig. 7-20. The shape of a famous (or infamous) green makes for a great clock.

One set of hands.
One set of hour markers.
One piece of green felt.

Instructions

1. Cut a football helmet in half.
2. Locate the position of the hand-shaft hole.
3. Drill the ⅜-inch hole.
4. Using contact cement, glue the green felt to cover the ¼-inch plywood that fits into the picture frame.
5. Attach the helmet to the plywood.
6. Insert the plywood into the frame.
7. Install the clock movement, hands, and hour markers.
8. Hang the clock by a conventional picture hanging device (Fig. 7-19).

GOLF CLOCK

Materials

One ¼-inch piece of plywood (approximately 10 × 18 inches).
One piece of green felt to cover the ¼-inch plywood.
One battery movement.
One set of clock hands to fit.
Twelve golf tees (any color).
One golf ball.
One small piece of black felt.
One handful of beach sand.

Instructions

1. Cut the piece of ¼-inch-thick plywood in the shape of a favorite golf green.
2. Locate the position and drill the ⅜-inch, hand-shaft hole.
3. Cover the plywood with green felt or velvet.
4. Cover a small area of the green felt or velvet with a thin layer of white glue. While the glue is wet, sprinkle on beach sand to simulate a sand trap.

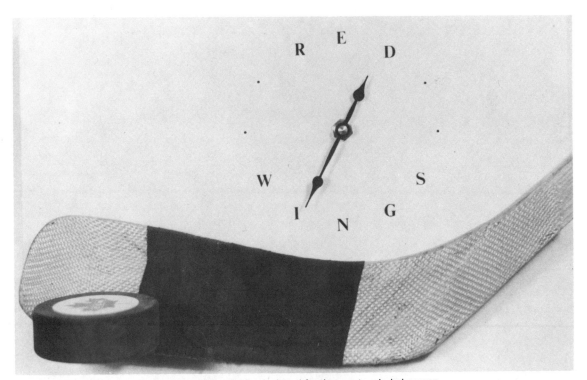

Fig. 7-21. The hockey clock is another of the clocks designed for the sports-minded person.

5. Drill a 2-inch hole somewhere on the green to serve as the cup.

6. Glue a piece of dark (black or brown) felt behind the hole.

7. At the hour marker positions, drill 12 holes. The holes should be large enough to permit a golf tee to be inserted through the plywood.

8. Glue the tees in position, and cut the tee ends flush with the back of the ¼-inch board.

9. Drill a 3/16-inch hole through the 1/4-inch-thick board, and a 1/8-inch hole into a golf ball.

10. Screw the ball onto the ¼-inch board with a flathead wood screw.

11. Install the clock movement.

12. Install the hands.

13. Hang by the bracket molded into the clock movement or by conventional means (Fig. 7-20).

HOCKEY CLOCK

Materials

One bottom portion of a hockey stick.

One hockey puck.

One ¼-inch-thick-by-12 inches-by-18-inches piece of plywood.

One piece of white material to cover the plywood.

One battery movement.

One set of hands to fit.

One set of hour markers.

Instructions

1. Screw the hockey puck onto the wood stick.

2. Cover the ¼-inch back with the white material.

3. Screw the hockey stick to the ¼-inch board.

4. Drill a ⅜-inch hole through the upper left-hand area of the ¼-inch-thick board.

5. Insert the movement.

6. Apply the hour markers.

7. Hang the clock by conventional picture hanging supplies (Fig. 7-21).

Chapter 8

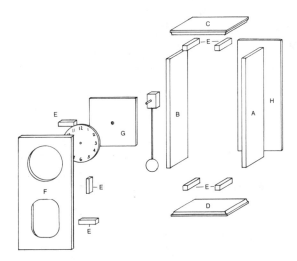

Selling Your Work

M OST CLOCK BUILDERS ARE BOTH BLESSED and cursed with their love affair with wood. They are blessed with the ability to transform raw wood into beautiful wood-clock cabinets. Yet often the same craftsman is cursed because creating fine clock cabinets is habit forming and results in a house full of handmade timepieces.

The average craftsman building clocks has produced so many clocks that his house has at least one of his works ticking away in each room. Also, most of his relatives and friends have been the happy recipients of his work.

Craftsmen tend to become so involved with the process of building clocks that they are compelled to keep building them whether the clocks have resting places or not. If this sounds familiar, the answer just might prove to be profitable. Why not sell your clocks? By entering the clock market, the craftsman has the opportunity to enjoy woodworking, but he also has the chance to make some extra money to help support his avocation.

SELF-ANALYZATION

Before venturing into the marketplace, the craftsman should ask himself certain questions. Do you have time to build in large quantities? The person who plans to engage in selling products of his shop should make a personal commitment and realize that his love of clock building could become more of a burden at times than a love. One example would be when a store owner makes demands that are difficult to meet.

Would you compromise the quality of your work to meet demands made upon your time? If this could become a problem, then the quality of the products produced could be adversely affected.

Before embarking upon the field of selling clocks ask yourself, "Why do it in the first place?" If the craftsman is entering the market intent on making vast sums of money, he had better reconsider this move. The sale of clocks on the market can be very rewarding, but not always extremely profitable.

The craftsman's shop should also be analyzed. Are the tools in the shop suitable for large-scale production? The craftsman primarily building with hand tools cannot produce clocks fast enough to sell at a marketable price. Power tools, preferably those such as stationary machines, are more suitable to mass-production techniques that can lower the amount of time required per unit.

Individual points to consider might include the possibility that the craftsman will work alone, with a partner, or partners. How much initial money will be needed to begin the venture? Can you afford to lose the initial investment? If not, the investment will not be a wise move.

MARKETPLACE ANALYSIS

The marketplace is another important consideration that needs to be surveyed prior to when the craftsman decides to sell the fruits of his shop. The major question is, "Where can the clocks be sold?" Without a method of presenting the clocks to the prospective customer, there is no need to produce them in the first place.

When you are thinking of a location for selling the clocks, many craftsmen first think of the major national department stores or discount stores. The problem with these stores, and many like them, is that the individual store usually has no power to purchase items that have not first been cleared through their central offices. Often, all purchasing for the entire chain is done at the company headquarters. Providing the home office is within a reasonable distance, contacting them might reward the craftsman with a sales contract but the quantity purchased on a national or regional basis might be so great that the craftsman could not possibly produce enough clocks fast enough. This is not meant to be a discouraging factor. There are many other places where your clocks can be marketed.

One of the most desirable locations for selling clocks produced in the home shop are craft and gift stores. This type of shop is usually locally owned and perhaps managed by the owner. The person the craftsman meets at the store is often the person who has the power to decide whether or not to buy. Another advantage with this type of store is that they are usually glad to be able to offer their customers a product produced in the area. This is especially true for shops in resort areas.

One disadvantage to these stores is that the shop will only purchase small amounts. Because gift or craft store merchandise does not sell very quickly, their demand past their initial order might not be very large. This is especially true in the tourist stores that are mostly confined to a specific season such as winter skiing, spring river rafting, summer sun and fun, or great fall fishing.

Another disadvantage is that the gift and craft stores will expect to buy the clocks from the craftsman at a price much lower than the craftsman would sell them for in order for the store to realize a profit. Be prepared to accept a price for your products that is lower than your concept of what the consumer will pay.

One way for the craftsman to realize more profit per clock and not raise prices or lower quality is to cut out the middleman and sell the clocks directly to the consumer. This can be accomplished only if the craftsman has access to the buying public. Arts and crafts shows, which are becoming annual events across the nation, might be just the avenue for the clock craftsman. These shows are generally set up where the artist/craftsman purchases the right to sell his goods at his price in a specified area. There is only a one-time charge; a commission on what is sold is usually not imposed upon the craftsman.

Information about arts and crafts shows can be obtained by reading advertisements in craft magazines or in newspapers. Probably the best source of information on upcoming shows is to talk to the craftsmen selling at a show. Those who sell at the shows generally follow the craft-show circuit from weekend to weekend all spring and summer. Although selling directly to the customer means more money for the craftsman, it also can mean a lot of time will need to be spent on selling the clocks rather than producing them.

Other places craftsmen can reach customers are flea markets where people sell almost anything from new products or crafts to anything found in the attic. Also in this category are individual or group yard sales where the garages, attics, and basements of America are emptied. The "treasures" they turn up are sold to others so that they can clutter up their garages, attics, and basements.

Many craftsmen are excellent woodworkers but terrible salesmen. When this is the case, the craftsmen should engage the help of another who has the traits he lacks. This person might be a professional salesman who calls on many retail outlets. In this circumstance, the craftsman needs only to concern himself with the production aspect of the business and keep up with the orders the salesman brings in. The salesman, however, requires payment for his efforts. The payment usually takes the shape of a percentage of the selling price of goods sold.

WHOLESALE METHODS

There are two basic methods of wholesale merchandising to retail outlets: outright purchase and consignment. The outright purchase is preferable for the craftsman because the store purchases the clocks and then assumes all risks. If the clocks do not sell, it is the store who owns them—not the craftsman. The store would then absorb the loss. This is the method stores use to purchase almost everything they sell.

The consignment method of wholesaling clocks is often of interest to the shop owner, but not necessarily the craftsman. Under consignment, the craftsman and store owner sign an agreement that states that the store owner will attempt to sell the craftsman's clocks at a price of the store owner's choosing. When the clock sells, the store then pays the craftsman a previously agreed-to price. As can be seen, the advantage of consignment lies with the store; they have nothing to lose and everything to gain. At a first thought, the craftsman might prefer to avoid a consignment agreement, but there are some distinct advantages for the craftsman.

A gift-shop owner might not want to invest money in a product that is produced in a home shop. The store is his livelihood; he makes his living by picking products that are sure-sell winners. A homemade product sold by the craftsman waves an imaginary caution flag. It is easier for the shop-

keeper to say no than to take the chance.

The same shopkeeper might leap at the chance to sell a locally produced product on a consignment basis (where there will be no monetary investment on his part). As the clocks sell, proving to be a profitable product, the craftsman could then request that the shopkeeper purchase future clocks outright.

THE COMPETITIVE EDGE

The craftsman who intends to sell his clocks must have a competitive edge so that his products will have a chance on the open market. One competitive edge is the ability of the builder to purchase supplies at a wholesale price, much the same as larger companies do. Wholesale prices are lower, and that also helps to keep the per unit price of the finished clocks lower.

Although wholesale clock companies require the craftsman to purchase large quantities, most clock mail-order companies listed in this book offer quantity pricing. They might offer, for example, a battery miniquartz movement at a given price for quantities of from 1 to 10. For quantities of 11 to 20, the price per unit would be lower, and larger quantities would, of course, have a per-unit price that is substantially lower than the 1-to-10 price.

The same type of pricing can be found for clock hardware and lumber. For that matter, if enough merchandise is purchased from a source, the price might be less than the single part price. Check with all the suppliers you deal with (even local lumberyards and hardware stores). These merchants are accustomed to selling a hinge or two at a time. They will usually be more than glad to sell a dozen or so at a reduced price.

Another competitive edge that the clock craftsman should take advantage of is the use of mass-production techniques used in industry. To mass produce any product, the first step is to build a prototype. A prototype is one model of a project, in this case a clock, that is completely built from scratch. The prototype should be built paying close attention to the methods that can be used to speed production. The prototype will require careful measurements and fitting of parts. Once the tedious fitting has been completed, the prototype parts can be used as a templet for future clock parts.

One hint for mass producing clocks is to plan ahead. For example, if you are going to make 10 units of a particular clock, make a list of how many parts will be needed to complete 10 clocks. While building the clocks, cut 10 of each part before going on to the next step. When assembling the clocks, put them together in assembly-line fashion (another mass-production technique). Assemble all 10 at the same time. For example, if the first step in assembly is to glue hypothetical parts B and C together, glue all 10 parts B and C together before going on to the next step.

Mass-production techniques are excellent methods to lower the amount of time spent per clock, yet keep the quality at a maximum. The craftsman should always have his eyes open for new or improved techniques that will help in clock-building endeavors.

As a woodworker, we build for many reasons. It might be just an enjoyable way to pass time, the desire to transform raw material into finished products, or the satisfaction the craftsman receives when he gives or sells one of his projects to another. One way for the craftsman to increase the latter is to sell the fruits of his labor. This not only provides money for future clock materials, but also provides an outlet for the craftsman.

The craftsman should look beyond the advantages of selling his clocks and consider the possible problems that might arise. The craftsman will be asked to wear many hats. He will not only be the manufacturer, but also the salesman, accountant, advertising executive, and market specialist—just to name a few. These problems might be easily hurdled or might pose impassable obstructions. That is up to each individual craftsman.

Suppliers

WHILE ENGAGED IN THE ART OF BUILDING clock cabinets, you will find it necessary to use many pieces of hardware, clock movements, dials, hour markers, and other pieces of clock-building paraphernalia. The local hardware or lumberyard will satisfy some requirements. Local hobby or craft shops also will be of help. They often sell a limited variety of clock movements and hands, but the majority of the materials needed by the craftsman are not locally available.

Luckily for the craftsman intent on building clocks, there are several mail-order companies that sell clock-building materials. This section offers the name and address of the best companies currently selling supplies useful to the clock craftsman. Most of the businesses represented are companies that sell primarily clock movements and related supplies. A few others retail a general line of woodworking supplies, while others are a fine source for hard and soft woods. Following the name and address of each company listed, there is a brief description of their product line.

Albert Constantine & Sons, Inc.
2050 East Chester Road
Bronx, NY 10461

Catalog price: $1

This company has a well-rounded general line of woodworking supplies. Examples of their materials are clock plans, hardwood lumber, veneer, quartz battery movements (with/without pendulum), dials, hour markers, finishing materials, and molding.

Barap Specialties
835 Bellows Avenue
Frankfort, MI 49635

Catalog price: $1

Barap offers a catalog filled with hard-to-find supplies, including clock plans, quartz battery movements, dials, woodworking tools, and finishing materials.

Clock Crafters, Inc.
P.O. Box 170
Sedalia, CO 80135

Catalog price: none

Clock Crafters' catalog includes a selection of clock kits, clock plans, battery quartz movements, dials, and hour markers.

Craft Products Co.
2200 Dean Street
St. Charles, IL 60176

Catalog price: 32-page, no cost; 100-page, $2

Craft Products sells a complete line of clock-related products, ranging from clock kits, plans, and some hardwood parts, to all styles of clock movements, dials, and hour markers.

Craftsman Wood Service Company
1735 West Cortland Court
Addison, IL 60101

Catalog price: $1

The Craftsman Wood Service offers a fine selection of general woodworking merchandise. Examples of their product lines are, clock kits, clock plans, a wide selection of hardwood lumber, veneer, battery and windup movements (with/without pendulums), large grandfather type movements, dials, hardware, and finishing materials.

Croy-Marietta Hardwoods, Inc.
P.O. Box 643
Marietta, OH 45750

Catalog price: $1

This company sells a wide selection of hardwoods in many sizes, grades, and species. They also offer kiln-dried turning squares and hardwood plywood.

Cryden Creek Wood Shoppe
101 Commercial Avenue
P.O. Box 18
Whiteville, NY 14897

Catalog price: $.50

Cryden Creek sells primarily hardwood lumber, turning blocks, woodworking tools, and woodworking books. One item of particular interest that Cryden Creek sells is preturned hardwood spindles which can be used as finals.

Educational Lumber Co., Inc.
21 Meadow Road
Box 5373
Asheville, NC 28813

Catalog price: $1 (refundable on order)

Educational Lumber sells a complete line of lumber, both hard and soft woods. Accessories they sell include dowels, screwhole buttons, and plywood.

Emperor Clock Company
Emperor Industrial Park
Fairhope, AL 36532

Catalog price: none

The Emperor Clock Company bills themselves as the world's largest manufacturer of do-it-yourself grandfather clock kits. In addition to their kits, they sell clock plans, windup movements (both large and small) and dials.

Esslinger & Co.
1165 Medallion Drive
St. Paul, MN 55120

Catalog price: $1 (refundable with first order)

Esslinger sells battery movements with or without pendulums, dials, and hour markers. They also have available quartz movements; inserts include the movement, dial, hands, and bezel all assembled and ready to insert into a slab, wall, or wood.

General Woodcraft, Inc.
100 Blinman Street
P.O. Box 1029
New London, CN 06320

Price list: no cost

General Woodcraft sells a fine selection of hard and soft woods. All lumber is kiln dried and available in small or large quantities. In addition, they offer woodworking tools, paneling, plywood, hardware, and adhesives.

Henegan's Woodshed
7760 Southern Boulevard
West Palm Beach, FL 33411

Price list: free with self-addressed, stamped envelope

The Woodshed sells a selection of cabinet and furniture-grade native American and imported hardwoods. Also, they offer the craftsman slab wood and turning squares. Of interest to the hobbyist is the fact that Henegan's Woodshed has no minimum order.

Kaymar Wood Products
4603 35th Avenue, S.W.
Seattle, WA 98126

Catalog price: no cost

Kaymar offers a great selection of hardwoods—both domestic and exotic—dowels, and veneer. Orders are custom selected to the customer's specifications.

Klockit
P.O. Box 629
Highway H North
Lake Geneva, WI 53147
Telephone: (414) 248-1150

Catalog price: $.75

Klockit offers one of the largest lines of clock materials available. They sell a wide variety of clock movements with and without pendulums. The movements may also be selected with many styles of chimes. Their movements range from the American-made miniquartz movement to the large grandfather-type movements, Many of Klockit's movements and dials are shown in this book. The majority of dials, hardware, and movements photographed have been supplied courtesy of Klockit.

Kuempel Chime Clock Works & Studio
21195 Minnetonka Boulevard
Excelsior, MN 55331

Catalog price: none

Kuempel has been owned by the same family for over 60 years. They sell a great selection of large grandfather movements. They also manufacture and sell their own clock kits and plans. The owners of this company seem genuinely sincere in their desire to assist the craftsman in any way they can.

Mason & Sullivan Co.
586 Higgins Crowell Road
West Yarmouth, MA 02673

Catalog price: $1
Mason & Sullivan Company sells a good selection of clock related materials. Their product line ranges from clock kits and plans, battery movements, large grandfather-type movements, and dials, to high-quality brass hardware. One interesting product they sell is a digital readout movement which can be used in the craftsman's designed cabinet.

Morgan (Bob) Woodworking Supplies
1123 Bardstown Road
Louisville, KY 40204

Catalog price: none

Morgan Woodworking Supplies sells a wide

range of woodworking materials. They sell wood-working tools, hardwood, veneer, brass hardware, picture-frame molding, finishing supplies, and woodworking books.

Native American Hardwood
R.D. #1
Box 6484
West Valley, NY 14171

Catalog price: $1

As the name indicates, this company specializes in native American hardwood and softwood lumber. The company offers the lumber in three grades of kiln-dried lumber. Native American hardwood helps the home craftsman by selling extra wide, and thin hardwoods.

Newport Enterprises, Inc.
2313 West Burbank Boulevard
Burbank, CA 91506

Catalog price: $2 (refundable with first order of $20 or more)

Newport offers a fine selection of clock merchandise. Their product line consists of a variety of clock movements, dials, and other clock related products. They sell clock kits, hardwood finals and frames, battery and windup movements, large grandfather clocks, dials, and hour markers.

Pacific Time Company
138 West 7th Street
Eureka, CA 95501

Catalog price: none

Pacific Time Company sells clock kits, redwood burl, battery quartz movements, dials, and hour markers. The movements they sell are pendulum and nonpendulum, and chime and nonchime. Pacific provides free hands (including second hand) and free numerals with the purchase of each movement.

Precision Movements
2024 Chestnut
Box 689
Emmaus, PA 18049

Catalog price: none

Precision Movements sells clock plans, pendulum and nonpendulum battery movements, dials, and hour markers. In addition to these basic clock supplies, they also sell epoxy resins for finishing, power tools, septarian stone slabs, and weather instruments.

Selva Borel
347 13th Street
Oakland, CA 94604

Catalog price: $2

Selva Borel offers one of the most extensive selections of clock supplies available in the United States. They sell clock plans, large and small, pendulum or nonpendulum, chiming or nonchiming battery, windup, and weight-driven movements, dials, and hour markers.

Sterling Hardwoods, Inc.
412 Pine Street
Burlington, VT 05401
Telephone: (802) 862-0186

Catalog price: free with self-addressed stamped envelope

Sterling sells a wide selection of domestic and imported kiln-dried hard and softwoods, veneers, woodworking tools, hardwood flooring, and custom millwork.

Talarico Hardwoods
Box 303 - R.D. 3
Mohnton, PA 19540

Catalog price: free with self-addressed stamped envelope

Talarico Hardwoods specializes in hardwoods. They also have highly figured and bookmatched lumber. Of special interest might be the sawn veneers they have available from ⅛ of an inch to 6 inches thick.

Timetric, Inc.
Box 296
Valley Road
Blue Bell, PA 19422

Catalog price: none

Timetric specializes in merchandising battery clock movements, dials, and hour markers.

Tremont Nail Co.
8 Elm Street, Box 111
Wareham, MA 02571

Catalog price: none

Tremont Nail Company is an excellent source for decorative nails for use as hour markers. They also sell hand-wrought, iron hardware.

Turncraft Clock Imports Company
611 Winnetka Avenue N.
Gidden Valley, MN 55427

Catalog price: $2.50 (refundable on first order)

Turncraft sells clock kits, clock plans, veneer, hardwood moldings, battery and windup clock movements, large grandfather-style movements, dials, and hour markers.

Unicorn Universal Woods, Ltd.
137 John Street
Toronto, Canada M5V 2E4

Catalog price: none

Unicorn offers over 80 species of foreign and domestic hard and soft woods and veneers.

Viking Clock Company
Foley Industrial Park
Box 490
Foley, AL 36536

Catalog price: none

Viking offers clock kits, battery, windup, and weight-driven movements. They also offer large grandfather-type movements, dials, and hour markers, and their kits as a finished product.

Weird Wood
Box 190
Chester, VT 05143

Catalog price: $.50

Weird Wood sells a wide variety of rare and unusual wood species. Many of their wood slabs are available with a clock movement cavity routed.

Westwood Clocks 'N Kits
3210 Airport Way
Long Beach, CA 90806

Catalog price: $1

Westwood offers a fine selection of clock kits, plans, movements (both battery and windup), large grandfather-type movements, dials, and hour markers.

Woodcraft Supply Corp.
41 Atlantic Avenue
Box 4000
Woburn, MA 01888

Catalog price: $2.50

The Woodcraft Supply Corporation offers the craftsman a good general selection of woodworking related tools and materials. Along the clock line, they sell clock kits, battery movements, both pendulum and nonpendulum, dials and hour markers.

The Woodworker's Store
21801 Ind. Boulevard
Rogers, MN 55374

Catalog price: $1

The Woodworker's Store sells a limited line of clock movements and dials, but they are an excellent source for hardware, finishing materials, and woodworking tools.

Woodworld
1719 Chestnut
Glenview, IL 60025

Catalog price: none

Woodworld sells a selection of hardwoods, veneers, and hardwood plywood.

Glossary

annual rings—Dark rings found in a log. They are formed by the tree growth.

backsaw—A handsaw with a heavy reinforced back to keep the blade straight. The saw has small, fine teeth to produce a smooth cut, and is commonly used for jointery cutting. An enlarged version is the miter-box saw.

bezel—A convex piece of glass covering a circular dial. The bezel has a metal ring around it with a hinge—so that it can be attached to the clock—but opened when necessary to wind a spring-driven movement or set the time.

bob—The weight on the bottom of a pendulum. The bob can be adjusted down or up, increasing or decreasing the pendulum swing, causing the clock to speed up or slow down.

book matched lumber—Sheets of thinly sliced veneer laid next to one another as if they were an open book.

brads—Small, thin, finishing nails.

brazing rod—A length of brass rod commonly used in a low temperature welding process called brazing.

butterfly hinge—A decorative hinge meant to be installed on the exposed surface.

butt hinge—A flat hinge that, when installed properly, is mostly concealed—leaving only the barrel of the hinge exposed. Large butt hinges are commonly found on doors.

butt joint—A wood joint where two boards meet and are glued without additional dowels, splines, or other methods, to increase strength. This is not an overly strong joint. If more strength is required, the joint must be altered or replaced.

campaign trunk corners—Metal corners once used on trunks to protect it from being damaged in transit. The campaign corners used today tend to be more of a decorative than functional nature.

chamfer—A diagonal cut on the end of a board from the top edge to the end of the board (not to the other edge). A cut from edge to edge is a bevel.

check—A crack in the ends of boards caused by uneven drying.

chisel—A tool that is ground to a cutting edge. It is used to cut or carve in wood.

coping saw—A handsaw consisting of a metal frame, a handle, and a thin, replaceable blade. The saw is designed to cut curves in thin wood.

countersink—A recess cut in wood so that the head of a flathead screw will lie flush or below the surface of the wood.

countersink bit—A drill bit specially designed to drill a shank hole and a recess for the screw head. The countersink bits are available in various sizes equal to the sizes of screws.

cove bit—A router bit designed for a concave cut on the edge of a board.

cut nails—Nails with a rectangular shank and head commonly used to nail wood to concrete.

dado—A groove cut into a piece of wood, not through, but across the grain.

dado blade—A type of saw blade that can be mounted on a table saw or radial-arm saw. The blade can be set to cut grooves of various widths and depths in boards.

deck cleat—An anvil-shaped device found on the deck of a boat. A line (rope) is tied to the cleat.

dial—A painted or printed piece of metal, wood, or paper, that serves to mark the hour locations. Dials are usually commercially produced.

dovetail joint—A joint that has interlocking fingers (square notches). This produces a very strong joint.

dowel—Wood cut to rod shape. The rod is usually available in 3-foot lengths and a variety of diameters.

edge rabbet joint—A joint commonly found on picture frames where the glass fits into a recess. It is an L-shaped cut on the edge of a board.

ellipse—An elongated circle—an oval.

escapement—A mechanism which allows the clock to evenly wind down.

final—A decorative, turned piece of wood found at the extreme top of the clock cabinet.

fit-up—A clock movement, dial, hands, and often a glass bezel assembled into one component part. The fit-up needs only to be inserted into a clock face.

flathead screw—A wood screw that has a flat head designed to be countersunk below the surface of the wood.

forming tools—Tools that are used to shape wood. Files and rasps are examples of forming tools.

furniture buttons—Wood plugs that are glued in a hole in the surface of a board. The button is used to cover the head of a countersunk screw.

gong strike—A clock movement that strikes once on the half hour and counts the hour on the hour. The movement might use one chime rod or it might incorporate two rods (which tend to produce a more even tone).

grid pattern—A method for reducing or enlarging a design. This method uses a system of squares drawn over the design. Another set of larger or smaller squares are drawn. The design is then plotted on the second set of squares.

grit—The method by which sandpaper is graded. The higher the grit number, the finer the paper.

hand length—The measure from the hand shaft to the tip of the minute hand.

hanging bracket—A metal or plastic bracket on the rear surface of a clock movement. The bracket is used to hang the movement on a wall. The bracket can be molded into the plastic movement case.

hardware—Nonwood parts not directly related to the clock movement. Examples of hardware include hinges and door pulls.

hasp—A hinged locking device used to hold a door closed.

hour-mark locator chart—A chart made of heavy cardboard used to locate the 12 hour positions of a clock face.

jointery—The technique of increasing the strength where two or more boards meet.

kiln-dried lumber—Lumber that has been dried

in an oven (kiln). The moisture content of kiln dried lumber is less than 10 percent. The less moisture the less chance of warping or checks (cracks) forming in the wood.

kiln-dried turning squares—Blocks of wood thick enough to be turned into bowls on a wood lathe. The wood has been dried in a kiln to reduce its amount of moisture.

lathe—A powerized woodworking machine that rotates the wood while it is shaped with a chisel.

lathe face plate—A flat piece of metal. One end is screwed to the wood to be turned and the other end is screwed to the lathe. This can be used when turning bowls or other similarly shaped objects.

mallet—A striking tool that resembles a hammer. The head, or striking surface, can be made of rubber, wood, or plastic.

Masonite—A trade name for building material made by reducing wood to its basic component parts. This composite is then subjected to heat and pressure. The result is an economic material with unilateral strength and many uses in the furniture and building industries.

masonry drill bit—A drill bit that is specifically designed to drill holes through masonry materials (brick, cement block, ceramic).

millwork—A general term applied to molding used in clock building. This also applies to the framing around doors and windows.

miniquartz movement—A clock movement with a very small exterior size. The miniquartz can be used in clock cases in which there is a limited amount of space available.

miter—A wood joint where two pieces of wood are fitted together at angles. For example, two boards cut at 45-degree angles will fit together to form a 90-degree angle.

miter box—A woodworking jig designed for cutting miters on wood.

molding cutting head—Three knives that fit into a holding device which is held on the arbor of a table saw. The knives may be replaced by various shaped knives which will result in the shape

being reproduced on wood.

mounting board—The board to which the dial or movement is mounted.

movement—A general term applies to the mechanism which operates the clock, regardless of the type of power used to run it.

octagon—A geometric shape that has eight equal sides.

pan-head screw—A wood screw with a flat head that remains above the surface after being screwed in.

parquet floor tiles—Preassembled wood squares cut to 12 inches by 12 inches. The squares are cemented on a floor to resemble a true parquet floor made up of several individual small pieces.

pendulum—The weighted shaft swinging from a fixed point. The pendulum is a method employed in some clocks to regulate the time. On others, it might be just for decoration.

pendulum length—The measure from the hand shaft to the lower most point of the pendulum.

pendulum swing—Refers to the distance the pendulum moves from side to side at its lowest point.

pilot hole—A small hole drilled in wood or metal. The small hole acts as a guide for a larger drill or wood screws.

plane—A hand tool that has a chisel type blade, used to remove wood in thin slices.

power saw—Any tool whose function is to cut wood or other materials—and is motorized.

quartz movement—A clock movement that relies on the ability of the quartz to vibrate at an accurate, even rate—thus dividing each second into small parts. This results in an accurate, reliable battery clock movement.

radial-arm saw—A motorized saw that uses a circular blade pulled across the wood being cut. The machine has been designed primarily as a cutoff saw, cutting against the grain.

recess—An area of wood that has been routed or chiseled away. The area is made lower than the surrounding wood. The recess can be cut to provide room for a clock movement.

roundhead screw—A wood screw with a round head that is not countersunk, but remains on the wood surface. This screw is used when the head of the screw is for decorative purposes.

rounding over bit—A router bit that is designed to cut a convex surface on an edge of a board.

router—A motorized tool that when used with various router bits, can decorate an edge or be used to remove or reduce wood in a given area.

sabre saw—A motorized, portable saw, useful for cutting curves in wood. It is often used to cut scroll work.

sandpaper—A thick paper onto which small abrasive particles have been glued. The particles vary in size from coarse, which removes large amounts of material, to extremely small, which produces a fine abrasive cut.

scroll work—Curved cuts with a sculptured appearance. This can be cut with a sabre saw.

septarian stone slabs—Slabs of stone that would create a distinctive desk or mantel clock when a clock movement or fit-up is placed on them.

shaper—A stationary machine whose function closely resembles that of a portable router. The shaper is used to cut the designs found in molding.

spring-driven movement—A wound-up spring provides the energy that operates the clock with this type of movement. The clock cabinet must be designed to provide easy access to the movement for periodic windings of the spring. Generally, the movement spring is wound with a key inserted through a hole in the clock dial.

stain—An oil- or water-based colored solution that is used to change the natural color of the wood for enhancement of the finished product. Stain-

ing must be done prior to varnishing.

stock—Wood or lumber.

Surform Tool—The trade name for a shaping tool used to remove large amounts of material.

table saw—A motorized saw that uses a stationary circular blade against which the wood is moved. The table saw has been designed primarily to cut in the same direction as the grain runs.

templet—A pattern that has been carefully drawn and cut out of cardboard, hardboard, or plywood. The pattern can then be traced several times.

timering—Circles drawn around the hours on a commercially produced dial.

varnish—A protective layer brushed or sprayed onto a wood surface. The varnish will dry to a gloss or satin finish.

veneer—Wood that has been sliced or rotary cut very thin (as thin as 1/25th of an inch). The veneer is then applied to other materials, usually of lesser quality.

weight-driven movement—A clock movement that relies on gravity to pull down weight shells hanging from the movement. This provides the energy that runs the clock.

weight shells—The decorative brass tubes that hang below a weight-driven clock. Empty weight shells can be suspended from any type of movement to resemble the weight movement.

wood rasp—A very coarse file used to remove large amounts of wood in a short amount of time; a forming tool.

wood screws—Screws used to fasten two or more boards together. Screws are used instead of nails when the parts might need to be separated at a later time or when a great deal of strength is required.

Index

Edited by Steven Bolt